JOEY

JOEY

JOE ALIBERTI

LitPrime Solutions
21250 Hawthorne Blvd
Suite 500, Torrance, CA 90503
www.litprime.com
Phone: 1 (209) 788-3500

© 2021 Joe Aliberti. All rights reserved.

No part of this book may be reproduced, stored in a retrieval system, or transmitted by any means without the written permission of the author.

Published by LitPrime Solutions   06/29/2021

ISBN: 978-1-955944-01-4(sc)
ISBN: 978-1-955944-02-1(hc)
ISBN: 978-1-955944-03-8(e)

Library of Congress Control Number: 2021913211

Any people depicted in stock imagery provided by iStock are models, and such images are being used for illustrative purposes only.

Certain stock imagery © iStock.

Because of the dynamic nature of the Internet, any web addresses or links contained in this book may have changed since publication and may no longer be valid. The views expressed in this work are solely those of the author and do not necessarily reflect the views of the publisher, and the publisher hereby disclaims any responsibility for them.

Contents

Chapter One 1

Chapter Two 18

Chapter Three 26

Chapter Four 31

Chapter Five 37

Chapter Six 45

Chapter Seven 47

Chapter Eight 53

Chapter Nine 56

Chapter Ten 60

Chapter Eleven 64

Chapter Twelve 71

Chapter Thirteen 75

Chapter Fourteen 81

Chapter Fifteen 87

Chapter Sixteen 93

Chapter Seventeen 96
Chapter Eighteen 100
Chapter Nineteen 103
Chapter Twenty 112
Chapter Twentyone 118
Chapter Twentytwo 121
Chapter Twentythree 129

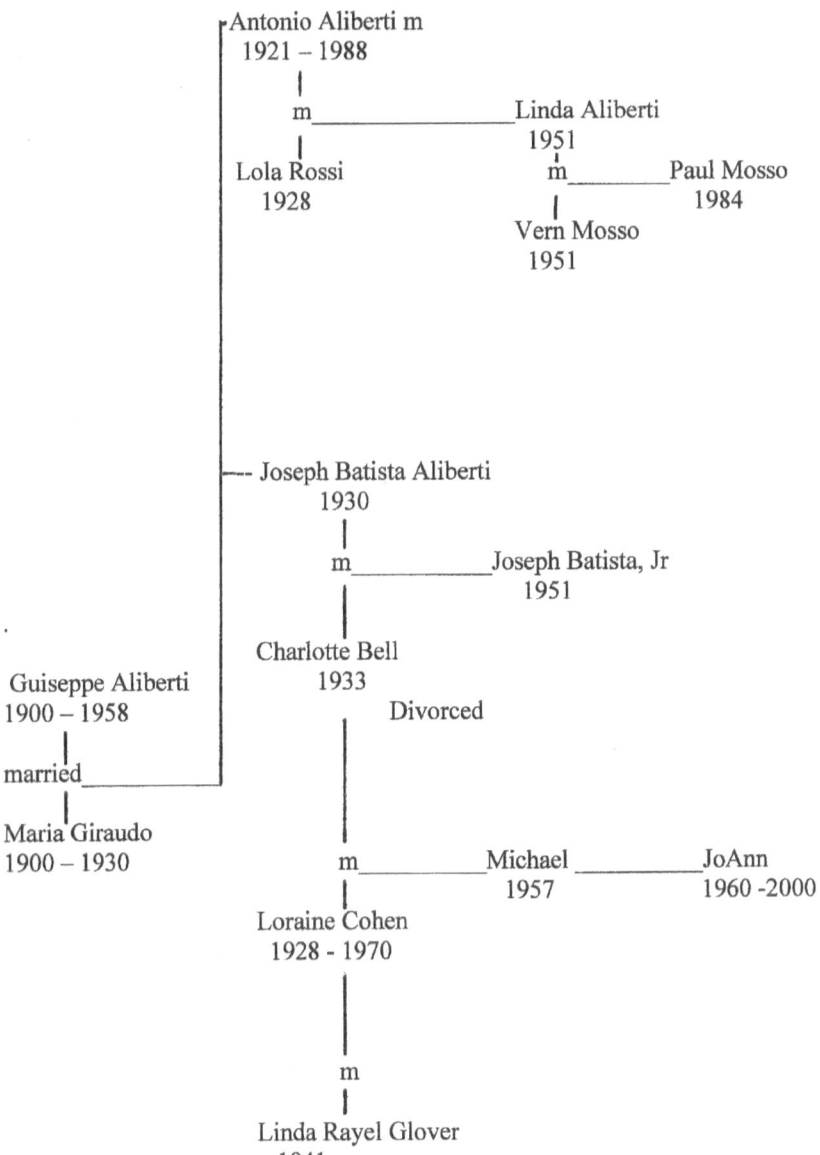

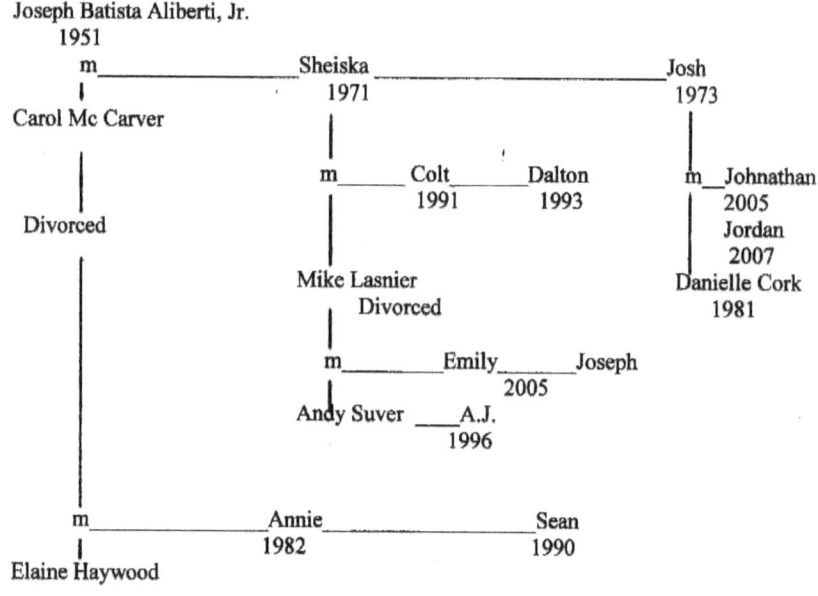

Joseph Batista Aliberti, Jr.
1951
m_____Sheiska_____Josh
                  1971   1973
Carol Mc Carver
                  m_____Colt____Dalton   m__Johnathan
                         1991   1993   2005
Divorced   Jordan
                                              2007
                  Mike Lasnier   Danielle Cork
                     Divorced   1981
                  m_____Emily____Joseph
                         2005
                  Andy Suver ___A.J.
                              1996

m_____Annie_____Sean
                  1982   1990
Elaine Haywood

Divorced

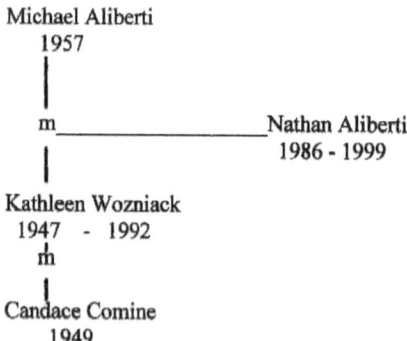

Michael Aliberti
1957

m_____Nathan Aliberti
                  1986 - 1999

Kathleen Wozniack
1947 - 1992
m

Candace Comine
1949

VIII

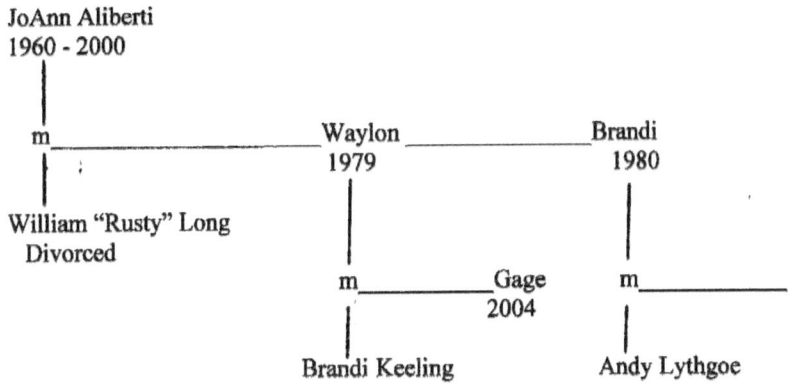

Chapter One

My story begins in the small town of Davenport, California population of roughly 300. My Mom and Dad were immigrants from Italy. Giuseppe was from Borgo San Delmaso a province in Italy approximately 5 km from the capital city of Cuneo and Maria Giraudo was from Vinollo in the Province of Cuneo, Italy. These two villages were about 4 km apart. Giuseppe courted Maria by riding his bicycle from his village to hers. Giuseppe was an only child and Maria had four sisters and three brothers. Before they married Giuseppe was a member of the Alpini a unit of the Italian army from the Piemonte region of Italy whose job was to protect against any invasion from over the Alps during World War I. During this tour he was captured by the German Army and was a POW for a period of about two years and was sent to a farm to work and fed a diet of potatoes three times a day. His weight went from 160 pounds all the way up to 185 pounds. After the war he returned to Borgo San Delmas and married Maria and started their family by having my brother Antonio in 1921. Because the Italian regime was in very dire straits my dad and Maria's brothers, Mike and Batista Giraudo, had the opportunity to leave Italy and to come by ship to America They came through Ellis Island and continued by train across country and landed in Davenport California where there are many brussels sprouts farms up and down the coast and they, all three, went to work for one. Their wages were only $50 per month including room and board. They worked there for several years until they decided to try sharecropping when it was offered to them by Louis Poletti. They grew brussels sprouts and artichokes and plowed the soil with a man held plow pulled by a horse. They grew great crops and when the crops were picked and shipped there was no market for them, they did not even make enough to pay for the crates or costs. They ended up filing bankruptcy.

Davenport had another industry the Santa Cruz Portland cement plant and both of my uncles were fortunate enough to get jobs there. The cement plant had a wharf that extended approximately ½ mile out over the Pacific Ocean. The cement could be shipped up and down the coast of California from this wharf.

My dad continued working in the farms for the $50 a month and room and board and my uncles moved to San Vicente Creek Road.

Although the population of Davenport was listed at 300 when you added the immigrant farmworkers and the cement plant workers the population grew to around 700 working in Davenport every day. Davenport was named for Captain Davenport who landed there in the early 1800s. The cement plant was built around 1908 and row houses around 800 sq feet each were built on Main Street south of the plant for the Greek Italian and Philipino families that worked at the plant and quarry. There were also three hotels that provided room and board.

The Southern Pacific Railroad had a depot station by the cement plant and a spur at the packing shed where the Brussels sprouts were packed. The railroad line ended in Newtown. The Greyhound Bus Company also came 3 times a day bringing the shift workers to the plant and delivering the mail to the post office. The road was only two lanes and was very narrow, twisting and turning with 3 wooden bridges that could only handle one car at a time. If two vehicles met at the bridge one had to wait.

Another industry in the mountain areas surrounding the town was timber harvesting.

During 1929 my dad was able to get his American citizenship

and with financial aid from Uncle Batista he was able to send for Maria and my brother Tony. Tony and Maria were living in a one room apartment in Italy where Maria took in laundry and Guiseppe sent her what money he could from America until they were finally granted a visa to come to the United States. They sailed from Italy to arrive at Ellis Island and then traveled across country by train to be finally reunited with Guiseppe in Davenport. The three of them lived in a rental house on San Vicente Creek Road. All of the cooking and heating of water was done on a woodburning stove. Tony started school at the Davenport Pacific elementary school when he was 8 and he couldn't speak a word of English. He did have two friends that lived next door John and Pete Pianavilla. I know very little more about this time in their lives. My mother Maria became pregnant with me and I was delivered premature at 7 ½ month on September 2, 1930 at Santa Cruz hospital. I was then hooked up to an incubator. Maria then started internal bleeding and it could not be stopped. Due to my premature birth and the complications from hemorrhaging and the loss of blood Maria passed away. Giuseppe lost his wife after less than a year and my brother and I lost our mother. Something I regret deeply even to this day. After a few months I was able to leave the hospital and I went to live with my uncle Mike and his new wife Aunt Velia in Santa Cruz. I lived with them for about two years and then my dad came and took me with him to Davenport to live with him and my brother Tony. They had moved into a home with another family the Manzones. The three of us lived in one bedroom. I really have very little recollection of this time. It was practical for two or more families to live together so that they could get by during the depression.

    The next thing I do remember is my father taking me to board with the Brovia family and that's when I acquired the nick name Joey. I was very young and did not like taking a bath so the only person I would let bathe me was their daughter Lena. After about a year, one early evening, my dad knocked on the door and with no explanation took me away. He carried me under his arms like a sack of potatoes put me in his car and we went back to the Manzone family to live in our one bedroom. We only had bathroom a little wooden outhouse with the standard wood carved half-moon design in the entrance door for light. At this period of my life became a very mischievous child. I got into a lot of trouble and it brought out the worst in my father's temperament. I was teased a lot by my brother and John Manzone and I ended up in trouble as I tried to fight back. It was during this time that I began to see the violent temperament of my father and I would end up with a beating. A beating not a spanking. Thank God for Mrs. Manzone, Nita. She really loved me and would intercede whenever she was able to stop quite a few of the beatings. It was obvious that I was not his favorite son because tony hardly ever got spanked, but I would get a beating approximately once a month. There were quite a few differences between tony and me maybe because he was born in Italy and spent his younger years there. He was very quiet and stayed mostly to himself because he couldn't speak very much English. I also believe he was afraid of our father and his temper. I had a lot of friends who teased me a lot so that I ended up in fights and in trouble with Dad. I spent a lot of my time during this period sitting in the little outhouse for an hour or so for my punishment. Nita was not only a great cook she was like my second mother. I do remember one time a hobo came and knocked on the front door to ask Nita for food. Even though we didn't have much she made him a couple of sandwiches which he took down to the old schoolhouse steps to eat. We could see him a block away from the house as he began eating the insides of the sandwiches and throwing the bread away. She was so upset she said she would never give another hobo anything to eat and believe me we did have a lot of hobos in Davenport that came by railroad. They lived in little huts along the railroad tracks in the Cypress grove across from the cement plant and in the eucalyptus trees above Newtown. They would come to homes and ask for food and jobs to make some money to help themselves. The way they dressed and looked was quite scary to us kids even though they never hurt anyone.

Guiseppe and Maria

Maria

My baby picture

Town of Davenport

We continued to live two families together. John and my brother decided to build a roller coaster with lattice and wings and a tail. It looked like an airplane. I was between 5 and 6 and they offered to let me take the first test ride. Not knowing any better I accepted and off I went down the first hill and then I was to go down the second hill which started in front of the church and ended up at San Vicente Creek Road. It was steep and I was going quite fast. The hand brake would not slow me down and I panicked and crashed into a ditch. The roller coaster was a mess and I ended up with a skinned up left arm and face. I went home crying and, of course, they ended up in big trouble with Mrs. Manzone. It took me two weeks to heal.

One night we were awakened around midnight and told to get out of the house because the house next door was on fire, so I went outside in our back yard in my long johns and a heavy coat. They thought that our house would also catch fire, but the house ended up with just some cracked windows from the heat. The other house burnt to the ground and we were able to return into the house around 5:00 A.M.

Around this period of time John and by brother went down to San Vicente Creek and met up with some other friends to do some target shooting with a 22 rifle at tin cans sitting on a 6' high grape stake fence. They were being supervised by an adult, Louis Betoil. John took his turn shooting and then he walked across the street to see how many cans he had hit and then it was my brother's turn. When John got through checking he said that he would stay down while Tony took his turn to shoot. Well, Tony took a while and John got impatient and rose up just as Tony pulled the trigger and hit John in the temple. He was rushed to the hospital and had emergency surgery to remove the 22 short slug that fortunately had not reached the brain. He returned home after several weeks and had to relearn how to speak. The doctors recommended that the two families no longer live together, so shortly thereafter the Manzone's moved to Santa Cruz and my father purchased the lot next door.

He hired a carpenter and a couple of handy men and they started building our new house. He charged all of the materials at the general store owned by Mr. Morelli and my dad made monthly payments. The house had a basement on the first level and four rooms on the second level two bedrooms, a living room and a kitchen. After we moved in a rear porch lean to was built containing a pantry, double laundry tray and a small bathroom. Then they built a porch off the kitchen that contained the ice box, kerosene stove and storage cabinets. The dining area had a view of the Catholic Church just below and from the open porch corner you had a view of the Pacific Ocean. The lower floor was an Italian style wine cellar, workshop and tool storage plus two additional storage rooms.

The garden area at the front elevation was approximately 1/2 acre and the back yard was approximately 1/4 acre and contained a chicken coup, rabbit pens and multiple pens for geese, turkey and guinea pigs. My dad was able to negotiate with the landlord for an additional acre next door and fenced this in for goats a cow and a pig pen.

JOEY

I would like to now describe the town and the coastal area and some of the people. As I mentioned before the population was around 300 including New Town and the town had only 8 streets. There were few businesses; among them were a French Bakery owned by Gilbert and Maria Ciaocca; a hotel owned by Pina and Frank Micosi; a blacksmith shop owned by Tony Libua; a general store owned by Mr. Morelli; a second hotel owned by Charlie and Carmelina Bella; a country store and lunch counter and gas station owned by Alvin and Elvicia Gregory. Later the Ciaocca's built a new building across from the Gregory's and sold bakery goods and had a lunch counter a gas station and mechanical repair shop. A packing shed was located across Highway #1 where they processed Brussel sprouts, broccoli and artichokes. There was a post office located in the General Store. The biggest industry was the Davenport Portland Cement Company built in 1906 employed quite a few people. They also had a quarry that produced the material for making the cement. There was also a jail built in 1914, but to my knowledge no one was ever imprisoned there. There was a butcher shop owned by Hugo (Ace) Bagnaco and Jim Bulaskaus.

At the end of Main Street was the Catholic Church, Saint Vincent De Paul just below our house. Milk came from the Jacko Cuclis Dairy on Swanton Road delivered daily except weekends by Ted Cuclis in a Model A Ford pickup. Sometimes, when my Dad was working nights, I would help Ted make the deliveries. One night we ran out of gas so Ted removed the gas cap but he couldn't actually see inside of the tank so he lit a match to see if he could see any better. The remaining gas, of course, caught fire. We got very scared and started pouring water into the tank, but the fire kept rising until it ran out the top. Thank God it didn't blow up. I left really quickly before his Dad arrived.

The Vomvolakis family had eight children, four boys and four girls, the largest family in Davenport. You can only imagine how hard it was during those hard times how hard it was to raise such a large family.

Charlie Bella's Ocean View Hotel

Charlie and Carmelina Bella

Original Davenport Cash Store and Post Office

Davenport Producers Packing Shed

Leonard Domenichelli and his son George with Jacko Cuclis

William Caiocca and sons Bill and Leo

Pacific Elementary School had 2 classrooms. Each classroom contained four classes, grades one through four taught by Hazel Thompson and grades five through the eighth grade taught by Anna Cook. There was also an auditorium. There was a large area for baseball and football, a front yard area with rings to swing on and a teeter totter. I started the first grade with Richard Dietz, Fred Moro and Ellen Cuclis. Since I did not speak English very well, I had a very difficult time reading. Italian was spoken almost all time at home. Once while I was trying to read "Roll over Red Rover" I had a very hard time. The rest of the kids started giggling and laughing out loud. I stopped reading so Mrs. Thompson picked up a yardstick and tapped me on the knuckles. Then she turned her back and I went over to the low window jumped out and went home. Mrs. Thompson sent my neighbor, Josephine Merlotti, to my house to get me to return to school. I was then held back a year and my new classmates were Billy Wilson, Joe Bearager and Thelma Micossi. The teachers were wonderful and did a great job of teaching us. If you misspelled a word in Spelling you had to write it ten times. In arithmetic Mrs. Cook made you add columns up and then down. This way if you added down and rechecked it down you could make the same mistake and would not catch it. The teachers had their work cut out for them because we boys were quite a handful. They were both dedicated and really did a wonderful job working with the ones that needed the most help. They gave the students who finished their work quickly additional work to keep them busy while the slower ones finished the assignment. One of the most wonderful things that they did was to have us all involved in a Christmas play for our parents. It was not a very easy chore for these teachers to find a way for all the students to participate, but they always made it happen and they got very good results. In summarizing my nine years at Davenport Pacific School I would have to say, looking back, that almost all of us who graduated would not change a thing.

The school furnished a football and baseballs, but not too many, we would use a baseball until we knocked the cover off and we would have to tape them up with tape we got from the telephone workers. A lot of times they ended up oblong instead of round. We played football with teams made up of six men (boys). We were not supposed to play tackle football, only flag football. But when the teachers didn't watch we played tackle football. One time we were playing flag football and Frank Olympio misunderstood and thought we were playing tackle football. I took the ball and ran around the end close to a bank and Frank tackled me. This was totally unexpected. I went down the embankment and sprained my ankle very badly. The bell rang and everyone went in and left me there. I decided to go home and soak it instead of going back to school. We only lived a block and a half so I hopped on 1 foot for a while and then would stop and rest and then continue. When I got to the neighbor's I was able to hang on to their fence while hopping. This really helped me get home and I began soaking the ankle. The teacher sent Josephine to get me to go back to school, but I told her no way and I would be back in the morning. I hobbled back to school the next morning, but there was no playing for me for the next week or so. I learned a good lesson about why the teachers did not want us to play tackle football. I particularly remember the time Billy Wilson and I got into an argument over a baseball game that ended up in a fight.

Billy was getting the worst of it and Mrs. Cook was trying to break it up. She told me to let him go and when I wouldn't she picked up a baseball bat and she started swinging it trying to hit my arms, but each time she would swing I would turn Billy and she would end up hitting him instead of me. We played a lot of games including cops and robbers which we played with wooden pistols that we made using clothes pins. Richard made one that actually looked like a machine gun. Billy used Richard's wooden machine gun and somehow dropped it and broke it. Richard chased Billy and we were sure he was going to beat him up. They ran around behind the school and we didn't really know what was happening. Instead of Billy getting beat up Richard came back holding his bloody nose and ran into the Boys rest room. I remember one fight Richard and I had during a ball game. The bell rang for us to go back in but we continued fighting until Mrs. Cook came out to stop us. Richard was furious because he was getting the worst of the fight. He started swearing and Mrs. Cook kept telling him to stop. He wouldn't stop and told her that his Dad was a Trustee of the Pacific School and that he could have her fired. Mrs. Cook had had enough she reached out and grabbed him by the hair and pulled him into the First Aid Room and poured liquid soap into his mouth. When she was done Richard ran home blowing bubbles all the way.

During these years I was given a couple of nick names "Potato Head" and "Garlic Head". I don't remember how Potato Head started, but I do know how Garlic Head started. I used to go home for lunch and one day I made a meat sandwich on French bread spread with "boniet" (garlic, anchovies, olive oil and parsley). After lunch I went back to school. My seat was right in front of Mrs. Cook's desk. She asked "Joey, what in the world did you eat for lunch?" So, this started a lot of teasing and more fights.

I remember the time the County School Nurse came to the school to give us vaccinations. Fred Moro was in line ahead of me and when he saw the needle he took off and ran home.

There was a 4H Club in Davenport and they used the school auditorium for meetings. We had a meeting one night that was exceptionally cold, but the auditorium had a furnace. I told our scout master, Francis Gregory, that I knew how to light it since Mrs. Cook had taught me how and I had done it before. I stared to light it and smelled gas but had no idea that was a problem. I turned on the pilot and put a match on the long rod and poked it through the hole to get to the pilot. As I put the match through the hole it blew up and knocked me backwards. I landed on the scout masters knees. The flames had hit me and singed my eyebrows, hair and the side of my face. Francis said we had better get me to emergency, but I told him I was fine. He told Abby Novelli who lived across the street to go get his car. As I started outside and the cold air hit my face and then I knew I was burned. It wasn't really that far to Santa Cruz, but I was hurting so badly that I kept yelling at Abby to go faster. It seemed like it took hours. At the hospital they put a salve on my face and drops in my eye. What a relief – it felt like an ice pack. I continued the drops and salve for about two weeks and was able to return to school in one week. My eye turned out o.k. but the scar on my face stayed for at least two years. The auditorium had wood sash windows and the explosion blew out 108 panes

My Dad worked two shifts at the cement plant so we would have marble games after school. One day I got into a game of Bull Ring with two brothers Ernest and Earl. They were trying to gang up on me and take some of my marbles as I was the "marble champ". Nobody else was around and I ended up winning all of their marbles and an argument started. Ernest and I got into a fight and Earl ran home to get a hand axe and was coming after me. He had me cut off from going home so I ran towards the cement plant through a turn style and over a wood walking bridge towards where my Dad worked. I went up a short hill to the plant dump and a man was working there and asked me what was going on. I told him and Earl was waiting at the end of the bridge. He asked me where I lived and then he grabbed a shovel and walked me home. Earl disappeared. I told the man that I would lock all of the doors. He waited a while and then left. In about five minutes Earl came to the gate so I picked up a four/ten shotgun and bullets and I came out on our second story porch put a shell into the chamber. I told him if he opened the gate I would shoot. After ten minutes of swearing he left. I was still plenty scared until my Dad finally got home. I was very lucky that that man was at the dump working. Have no idea what could have happened to me had he not been there. I thanked him and I know he told me his name, but I was so scared I don't remember it.

The school playground was used as a playground after school hours and on weekends for kids and parents alike. On many occasions most of the mothers would come out of their houses and call their kids home for dinner. No one ever called me I really missed not having or knowing a Mom. I shed many a tear and I still think about her to this day.

Chapter Two

My Dad did all of the cooking, so I had many chores after school to help him. I had to start the wood stove to heat water so he could bathe when he got home. Then I had to clean and prep the vegetables. I had to feed the animals which took about an hour and a half and then we would sit down for dinner. Then my bother Tony and I did the dishes Saturday consisted of working in the garden. Spading and weeding. The planting was done by our Father. Tony and I would sweep and mop the floors. We took our laundry to Mrs. Manzone in Santa Cruz.

Our main source of food was our huge garden and our animals. Even though times were tough I remember sharing vegetables, eggs and rabbits with our neighbors the Arvales family and the Merlotti family. Nick Arvales worked on the Brussel Sprout farms and had a very interesting side job. He bought and sold livestock. When Dad was ready to buy a pig, calf, or goat, etc. Nick would find one for him and deliver it to him. I spent many evenings at their house listening to the "Lone Ranger and Tonto", "Fibber Magee and Molly" and "Mr. and Mrs. North" with their children Pete and Irene. Mrs. Arvales baked excellent Greek pastry's and always had a plate for me that was exceptionally good.

Mario Merlotti worked at the General Store delivering groceries and later went to work at the cement plant while his wife Lena stayed home and cared for the children. I look back and remember that she was the most organized person I have ever known. They had three daughters, Josephine, Marian and Donna all born six years apart. Lena's mother, Rosie Russalelle also lived with them. They were wonderful to me. They occasionally went to a movie and they included me. And I would spend almost every Friday night at their home playing Monopoly. Some weekend evenings we played hide and seek. Lena was constantly working on the family budget especially for their annual family vacation. They would load up their trailer and camping gear and head for Silver Lake for a whole week. Their car was a 4 door Oakland, black with spoke wheels and I thought it was pretty snazzy.

Now that you've met the neighbors it's time to tell you about the Aliberti household. Tony had a very tough time. He had to learn English and he didn't have many friends to play with. I, on the other hand, grew up in Davenport so I had plenty of playmates. This presented a problem for me on Saturdays we had chores that lasted quite a few hours into the afternoon. All of my friends were playing at the school yard all day. I would try to coax my brother into letting me go play and then I would come back and do the work. He always told me that "If you go ahead and go "I will tell Dad". I became really frustrated and fumed about why I had to do all of this work and my friends didn't have to. I decided my Dad was the meanest man on the planet. After several Saturday's I decided to go play any way and sure enough my brother told Dad and I got a really good beating. I tried to get Tony to explain to Dad to get him to understand, but he would not do it. This created warfare because in my mind they were both against me. I continued to look for a chance to take off just to show them, but I always ended up with another good beating. Because of our age difference we didn't spend many years together.

Dad started a wood cutting business on the side. He cut wood to sell to the people with wood burning stoves. One source of the wood was in Bonny Doon It was Oak and Madrone. It came in long lengths and Dad purchased a truck so that we could take it to Davenport. Many Saturdays we would load, haul and unload wood.

He also got wood from Swanton on property owned by Mr. Morelli. He paid stumpage at the rate of $1.50 a cord. Dad and Tony used a two-man crosscut saw to fall the trees. You can just imagine the thud when one of them came down. I cleaned up the limbs and the brush. Occasionally we would see deer and quail. When Dad worked at the plant on Saturdays, I would have to help Tony cut the trees into 4' lengths by using a cross-cut two man saw. I could barely do it and I would get tired and couldn't keep my end up. I was only 10 or 12 years old. Tony would get mad and kept saying "I'm going to tell Dad". I told him to go to Hell and tell Dad that I was doing the best I could. It registered, he never told Dad. After we cut the tree into 4' lengths it was split into pieces by a sledgehammer and metal wedges.

Around this time Tony was going to Santa Cruz High School and he got the idea to make a canon wood splitter in his machine shop class. It looked like a steel rod about 18' long and 1 ½" around. The front was milled down into a cone shape with a hole drilled in about 2" round. At the end of the 2" hole he drilled another hole ¼ inch from the top. It worked by putting black powder in the front hole and then put newspaper as a plug and Tony would take a sledgehammer and drive the cone end into the middle of the cut log and then he would place a heavy piece of wood at the end of the cannon that acted as a back stop. Then he took a 6" piece of fuse and put it into the 1" hole and lit it. We ran about 30 feet away and when it went off it blew the log into four to six pieces. What a great invention. It saved many hours of hard work. Later he built an additional drive shaft for the star car that we had. He also built a saw and platform on the backend of the car. He could drive the car anywhere and unhook the car drive shaft and then hook up the drive shaft he made for the wood saw. We took the longer lengths and cut them into wood stove length. Tony would do the cutting and a second person would grab the cut piece and throw it into a pile. This was not a very safe thing to do as Tony did cut his wrist one time changing the circular blade and needed stitches. The wood cutting lasted for around three years. Tony was in his senior year and had enough credits to graduate by going only part time to school. He first got a job working swing shift at the Cement Plant and then when World War II started joined the army air corps and became a mechanic.

I now realize what great things he did in his life. Coming here from Italy into Ellis Island and traveling by train cross country with our Mom at such an early age. Learning English, Graduating from High School with vocational honors and best of all being smart enough to avoid confrontations with Dad. He was only whipped once. I really felt my life with Dad was pretty miserable. He more or less blamed me for my Mom's death and it seemed like there was nothing I could do to satisfy him. I really resented him for making me do so many chores at the age of 7 or 8 and kept me from playing with my friends. The only thing that I did that I didn't get into too much trouble for was preparing the vegetables. In his opinion, I could never feed the animals correctly and would end up with another spanking. I also had the chore of cleaning up the manure and putting it into piles to be used as garden fertilizer. I really had problems with the pig pen which was wet and sloppy. I had to wear rubber boots to clean it and I didn't even have a mask on, not too exciting.

I had to turn the soil in our large garden almost every Saturday. On the Saturdays he didn't work at the plant and was home I had no choice but to dig and listen to all my friends playing in the school yard. On the Saturdays he went to work I would try really hard to ignore them. Once in a while it got the best of me and I would leave and go play even knowing what the end result would be. He had a method of turning the soil that you had to follow. First you had to clear out a grassy area of about two feet wide, and then turn the soil which created a trench that you would put the weeds and fertilizer into and continue on. No matter how hard I tried I never satisfied him, and I would end up getting a spanking. It was at this time that I started thinking about running away. I actually went to our back door three times, but I was too afraid to take off. When I finally did go and came back I, of course, got the expected spanking. The next time I got up the nerve to go I went across the street about 200 feet from our house and hid in the outhouse of the barrel factory buiding. Most of Davenport was looking for me and my two uncles came from Santa Cruz to help find me. I could hear them all calling "Joey", but I wasn't about to come out. About 11:00 P.M. guess who opened the door? My Dad, of course, and he took me home and sent me to my room. I could hear my uncles giving my Dad Hell and asking him what was going on and what was he going to do? Dad told them that he wouldn't beat me, so they left. After about ten minutes he opens my door and beat me with a rope. I not only hurt physically for several days I was also emotionally hurt.

The first time I really ran away was over a job my Dad ordered me to do. There was a large pile of manure that he told me to spread in the garden and it had to be done by the time he got home from work or I would get another beating. I was freaked out by the size of this pile because I only had a little shovel and my little red wagon. I loaded up my little wagon and started spreading, but after a couple of hours I knew I couldn't get it all spread. I panicked and decided to run away. I cleaned out the wagon and put clothes, a bottle water and my Abraham Lincoln bank in it. I gave some of my play cars and truck to my friends and took off. I was planning on going to my Uncle Mikes in Santa Cruz by going down Highway 1. The town crier system kicked in and the word got to Charlie Bella that little Joey had run away. I had only gone about a mile and a half when Charlie came in his touring car with his daughter Gloria to take me back home. I got a big rock and ran up the hill and told him not to come after me or I would throw it at him. He convinced me to tell him what this was all about and talked me into going home.

While I was attending Mission Hills Junior High School, I asked for permission from my Dad to play in our championship baseball game against Branciforte Junior High School. He said no. The day of the game I told my teammates that I could not play. Their response was that I was the pitcher and how badly they needed me. I was really scared, but my final decision was that I couldn't let my team down. I pitched the game of my life. We shut them out and won 3 to 0. My brother had returned from the service and was working for the Lincoln Mercury Dealership and the game got over early enough to catch a ride home with him. All he kept saying on the way home was that I was really going to get it from Dad and that he told you not to play I tried again to get him to talk to Dad to explain to him and he said no way and just kept saying that I was really going to get it. We reached home I got out, opened the garage door and then decided I didn't want another beating and ran. I headed out about three blocks to a little shack built by Mike the tramp on the other side of the railroad tracks behind the packing shed where I worked. It was a tiny shack about 8 x 10 made out of wood he had salvaged from the Davenport dump at the end of the beach. It had a makeshift wood burning stove and a built-in wooden bunk and you could lie on the bunk and see the moon shining through the cracks. When I got to the shack it was so cold that I went back home to get blankets. The window to our bedroom was unlatched so I snuck through and got the blankets and took off. This was the first day of my 12-day run away. The next day I cut school and went back to the house to get more clothes and helped myself to some canned goods and got a lock and chain to lock my stuff up. I had some money from working at the packing shed so I developed a routine. I caught the bus to school and would bathe during gym class. I didn't take the bus home after school. I would get something to eat and then go to the Boys Club until 9:00 when they closed. Then I would go around the corner and take the 10:45 bus that took the workers for the swing shift at the cement plant. I would not get off in Davenport but would go to the cement plant and then would walk down the railroad tracks to my shack. I thought that they would not find me, but about five days later while I was in school my Dad and Tony found out where I had been staying and they broke in and took most of my food. The next day I cut school again, went to my house, found a window I could open and got in. They had put my food in the back seat of Tony's car, but it was locked so I couldn't get in. I decided I would fix him and went into the house, got some wooden matches and used them to let all of the air out of his tires and left. Tony told me later that he thought about tying a rope around my shack and pulling it over. On the 12th day Charlie Bella came over with a message from my Dad that if came home he would not beat me. I debated and finally concluded that since Charlie Bella said it would be ok it would be ok. I went home and I did not get a beating. Boy was it nice to get back into my bed and such a relief that he didn't beat me this time.

This was a turning point. Things did get much better, although he still beat me occasionally. It didn't stop until I turned seventeen and obtained a driver's license. Now I could borrow the car once in a while. I asked my Dad if I could use the car for a school dance a week ahead of time. I had a date that I was very excited about. He said yes but gave me a very long list of chores to do during the week. I can't really remember what I didn't do right during this week, but when the night came for the dance Dad said no to my using the car. I got so mad that I told him he could stick his car you know where and continued to tell him that if Tony had asked him for his car, he would have given it to him filled with gas. He started toward me and I reached over and grabbed him by his shirt chest high, sat him down on the couch. Then I told him that if he laid another hand on me I would kick the you know what out of him. I told him from now on to tell me what he wanted done and I would try my best to do it, but no more beatings or I would fight back. Then I let him go and told him again he could stick his car you know where. I left and went to the Ocean View Hotel and played pool. This cleared some of the air between us. I tried harder and he got off my case a bit. It wasn't perfect or a love affair, but at least the beatings stopped.

Virginia and Lena Brovia

Chapter Three

Every year Dad would butcher an approximately 500 lb pig with the help of close friends Julio Belli, Mike Falco and my two Uncles Bob and Mike Giraudo. This process took 2 days. The first day was the kill and the cleaning of the hair by using hot water and burlap sacks. My job was to stoke the wood stove fire for the hot water. They then hung the pig to let it dry out overnight. The second day they did the butchering. The part that was to be used as bacon was cut up into pieces, salted and put into 5gallon crocks. A section of the basement was turned into a drying room for the salamis and sausages to cure in. The casings for the salami and sausage were made from salted intestines from cows, salted which had to be soaked and cleaned. They used a hand meat grinder to grind all of the ingredients and with a special attachment filled the casings. By Sunday evening the salamis and sausages were hung in the drying room to dry and everything was cleaned. After the curing everyone who worked on this got a package of the meats. Some of our neighbors were also the recipients of a package.

The drying room was also used for drying mushrooms. During mushroom season, in October, Dad and I went to Bonny Doon up in the mountains about 7 to 8 miles from our house to pick mushrooms. We used a 25 lb. sprout barrel with a shoulder strap to put them in. We picked them from under the Oak and Madrone trees. The ones under the oaks had a brown top and the bottom side was off white. The ones under the madrones had a reddish top and the bottom a light green. They grew best after the early fall rains and on the side of the mountain where the sun hit. On this particular day our timing was perfect – there were mushrooms galore. The large ones were easy to spot, but the smaller ones had to be picked from under leaves that we lifted with a stick and then we picked them. The large mushrooms we dried and used for cooking. The small ones were for fresh eating but could also be dried. My Dad had two sprout barrels and I had one and they were all filled to the brim. On my way down the hill slipped on some leaves and my barrel full of the mushrooms went rolling down the hill. I got a couple of back hands from my Dad and with tears flowing I began salvaging what I could. A few of the small ones were saved for meals and the rest were sliced and put on flats with cheese cloth and put on racks in the drying room for about two months when they were ready to be cooked and used for pasta sauces.

We always had food on the table even though these were very poor times because of our huge garden and all of our animals. Some of the best meals I ever ate, even to this day, was a dish Dad called German Pasta made with potatoes and homemade sausage. Another was pan fried rabbit and another was tripe. His minestrone soup was as good as or better than any I've ever eaten. Crab salad that he made sometimes on Sundays was made with artichokes, asparagus, tomatoes, etc. The crab was sprinkled over the vegetables and then sprinkled with lemon juice. He boiled beef and stew meats and used a sauce of garlic, anchovies, parsley and olive oil to spruce up the flavor. He also used it on boiled chicken and as you already know I put it on sandwiches. The most exciting meal that I remember was when we had T-Bone Steaks. Dad would take three cast iron frying pans and put olive oil and garlic in two of the pans. When the oil was hot he put the seasoned steaks in and in the third frying pan he cooked French fries. He got warm sourdough French bread from Ciaocca Bakery and we would soak up the steak/olive oil and garlic juices. Mama Mia! I remember it to this day.

We had the General Store which carried food, clothes, shoes, hardware etc. It was a great store for our little town of Davenport. Once a month my Dad would make a trip to Santa Cruz to get animal feed, chicken feed and barley. He would also stop at Zoccolis Italian Deli for cheeses, Italian cold cuts, pasta etc. He would sometimes stop at Pure Food Center Market for some special meats.

Saint Vincent de Paul Catholic Church that we viewed from our Dining Room.

Davenport Pacific School

The whole school enrollment. Little Joey is in the top row 2nd from left..

Chapter Four

Tony left to fight in World War II when I was only eleven years old. I was called the "orneriest kid in town". I guess I have to agree with their assumption. In my defense no one really knew what my home life was like. Maybe a few knew, but they never did anything about it. Since my Dad worked swing shift at the cement plant and I had didn't have a babysitter or adult supervision I went home alone to do my chores and then would have dinner by myself. I will say there was always something for me to heat up and eat. I did spend some evenings with the Arvales family listening to the radio and Friday evenings with the Merlotti family playing Monopoly. It was very scary when I went home alone. At 10:00 I had to light the wood stove so that Dad would have hot water when he got home from work around 12:15. The house would creak during the winter and the plum tree outside my window rubbed the house when the wind blew. A few times I got so scared that I would get up and get a butcher knife and put it under my pillow. I really don't know what I would have done if someone actually came in. One good thing that happened during all of this was at the start of baseball season I could get the San Francisco Seals games on the radio and could listen to hear how my hero Joe Brovia (a Davenport Hero) was playing. I did, however, get into trouble several times because I would fall asleep listening to the game and the radio would still be on when he came home. So, as usual, I got a few smacks. During this time spent a lot of time alone.

When I got a little older the Ocean View Hotel became my favorite hangout because of its pool table. When the table was not in use Charlie Bella would let us play. Our time limit was 8:30 and then we had to go home. It was very scary for me going home alone. I would walk to the end of the main street and then I would run as fast as I could up the hill to our front gate. It seems kind of silly to be so afraid, but as I have mentioned we did have hobos in town.

Sometimes on Saturdays I would go alone trout fishing in San Vicente Creek. Trout season opened around the first weekend in May. One year I decided to go a week early, which is called poaching and against the law. I walked a mile and a half up the Creek and stopped at a spot where I could see quite a way up and down the creek. I was really excited because I had caught six trout when I heard a noise. I looked right and saw the game warden's high boots and green pants. He yelled at me "Hey, young man". The creek was shallow, so I waded across it with my fish. I started up a steep hill which was covered in brush which helped to hide me. He kept yelling out to me, I kept going up the hill. There was no way he could catch me. The brush hid me and my tracks. I got away from him got to the top of the hill and I walked on the cement plant railroad tracks and went home the back way. The following week I was playing pool at the hotel when Charlie Bella opened the ticket window and motioned for me to come into his office. He closed the door and asked me if I had been fishing at San Vicente Creek. I, of course, told him "no, not me". Mr. McDermott, the game warden must have stopped by and described me to Charlie because he knew quite well it was me. He said "Don't lie to me" so I confessed and told him that it was me. He gave me a good reprimand and I promised him I would never do it again. That was the end of that.

While on the subject of fishing I would like to tell you about the Filipino farm workers. Our beach has two rock ledges at each end and the Filipinos used to fish off of them on weekends. They wrapped a line around a coffee can with a hand grip on the end of the can. I decided that I wanted to try this, so one Saturday I took a coffee can from home and put a wood handle with a nail on each end to secure it and went to the General Store to buy line, hooks and sinkers. I used mussel worms for bait. I got these by prying the mussels loose with a flat bar from the rocks. I baited my hook and grabbed the line by the sinker, twirled it like a lasso and let it fly. Off it went coffee can and all. I forgot to hold onto the handle. There went my whole fishing outfit sailing into the Pacific Ocean. With tears in my eyes that was the end of my first ocean fishing experience. I did try it again later on and it was exciting as I caught several ocean sea trout about a foot long and they very good eating.

I also started hunting quail at the Sprout Patches area and ducks at the ranch ponds with a 410 shot gun. I would also go out onto the ocean bluffs and shoot at sea gulls with a 22 rifle. There was a rule for shooting at the sea gulls. You could only shoot at them going down wind. I don't think I ever hit one. Sometimes my buddy, Richard Dietz, would go hunting with me. I must now confess that I did something I am really not proud of. Ammunition was very expensive and there was no way I could afford it so I would put on a trench coat and go to the side room of the General Store and put shells into my pockets. Again, I admit that I am not proud of this.

Life during this time consisted of school, dinner, dishes and Dad and I watching the T.V. sitting on two canvas lawn chairs. On Friday nights we would go to visit his friends. Tony Luba {who was the town blacksmith} and Giovani Orlando his neighbor. I was like their mascot and I would sit there for around three hours as they drank homemade wine. They talked and I listened to their war stories. Occasionally one or the other would get really loud to get their point across. Giovani talked about his wife and sons who were still in Italy and how one day he wanted to bring them here to America. As it turned out he eventually, many years later, did bring them here. They unfortunately ended up divorcing and the sons would have nothing to do with him. Other times his buddies would come to our house. Dad drank very lightly during the week, so he really made up for it on the weekends.

He had a permit to make 200 gallons of wine per year for home consumption. The 200 gallons didn't last out the year so to get around this he would get an additional permit for his friend Julio Belli, who didn't drink. To make it official he put up a wall and put his 200 gallons on one side and Julio's on the other side. This still didn't make it the whole year and he would end up buying several cases of gallon bottles of wine. He bought his wine grapes from Joe Bertoli's vineyard in Bonny Doon. He brought the grapes and put them into a grape crusher that was backed up to a large redwood tank in our back yard. He then put a round redwood 1 x 6 lattice into the tank, put on boots and stomped down as far as it would go. Then he put cleats to hold it down and the top was put on. He checked for sugar content in the next two to three weeks. When the wine was deemed ready, he put a hose on the spigot and ran the first wine into prepared barrels. Then he took the pulp and put it into a press and used a screw jack every day and added wood blocks until the process was complete. This was the second wine. A third wine was processed by adding water to the remaining pulp. This resulted in a lighter wine and was the first to be consumed. He also made grappa from the pulp. He made his own still and it turned out around 150 proof alcohol. One Saturday night three of my buddies and I decided that we would go the Santa Cruz Boardwalk and try to meet some young ladies. I told them that I would steal some of my Dads Grappa. Hoping we would not get caught we went onto the beach to drink the grappa. We had about half a fifth in the bottle and we passed the bottle around until we had less than half left. We got pretty drunk, so we went and sat on the steps leading up to the Boardwalk for three to four hours trying to sober up. Needless to say, all of the young ladies were nowhere near close to being bothered by any of us.

I was always like my Dad's mascot and he would sometimes take me with him to play Frogo with his friends on Saturday nights at the

Ocean View Hotel. This was a card game similar to Pinochle. They played for drinks. Every month one of the two hotels would have a dance and it was really a thrill for me to go with him to watch. I remember watching Mr. and Mrs. Brovia dancing. He would kick up his right heel and I thought this was really funny because no one else ever did this. You could tell that he really thought this was great just by the way he looked. One night we left and started up the hill to our house. There was an outside wedding reception for the Brovia's daughter and new son in law. A relative, her cousin, who worked with my dad spotted us and asked Giuseppe to come on over and have a drink. He poured a glass of whiskey that looked like about three shots. We left after a half hour and we started home. We got halfway home when he started weaving. I grabbed him by his arm to steady him. It took all of my strength to get him the rest of the way home. I took him to our back door because there was no way I could get him up the stairs to the front door. I got him into the kitchen but we both couldn't go through the door at the same time, so he slipped away from me and stumbled into the refrigerator and went down. It was really a good thing he had been drinking because he didn't break any bones. I tugged and pulled and finally got him into bed. Another time we were leaving the Ocean View Hotel after an evening of playing cards and drinking he started weaving. The W.P.A. had been putting in sewers in our community and the ditch they had dug was left open with no barricades. The dirt was piled on the opposite side of the streetlight and it made a shadow, so it was very hard to see. He weaved too much and down he went into the ditch. Again, thank goodness he had been drinking because he only ended up with bruised ribs and had to use mustard plasters for a week or so.

The Hotel Ditalia had a room with three slot machines. I used to try to sneak in to watch the people playing. I would quite often be run out. There were two iron doors that pulled up to hide these three slots because they were illegal. One time I didn't see anyone there, so I went in and looked for any money that could've been dropped or left behind and I started pulling the handles of the machines. To my surprise the dime machine played so I kept playing it. After a dozen pulls or so three plums came up and paid fourteen dimes. In my pocket they went and out I went.

Basketball team. I'm the one on the end lower right.

Chapter Five

At the age of twelve I got my Social Security Card and started working a seasonal job at the Davenport Producers Association owned by Louis Polleti. They shipped Brussel sprouts, broccoli, artichokes and other vegetables. When World War II started Tony and others his age were drafted into service creating a shortage of workers, so I was able to get a job. Braceros from Mexico were brought in to help and given their green cards. The first couple of years my job consisted of bringing the sprout drums to the assembly line and putting a scoop of ice on top of the sprouts after they were put into the drums. I made $.35 an hour. Now I could start buying my own school clothes and look like the rest of my friends instead of wearing the bib overalls that my Dad kept buying for me. The third year my job was loading the drums into the railroad cars. Sometimes the orders would be mixed with a row or two of broccoli and/or lettuce from Salinas packed in crates. They had to be stacked three crates high and for me to get the third one up I had to get a running start and with a knee bounce I barely got it up. One time I missed the last crate and the compressed lid popped open and lettuce flew everywhere. Our boss, Curly, came and boy did I catch hell. With his help we picked up the lettuce and finally got it loaded. The fourth year I was older and strong enough to handle all the different jobs associated the packing shed operations.

Brussel sprouts were the largest crop and accounted for 80% of the packing and shipping. They came from different ranches in drum barrels or crates and were unloaded on wooden platforms then taken by weight lifts to a conveyer where they were sorted by five women. They were then dropped into hampers that were on scales and then the hampers were put into a pre cooler four across and run thirty feet through ice cold water and then dumped into the barrels with a scoop of ice on top and the lid nailed on. Then they were loaded into the railroad cars. Saturdays were the big days for packing when we usually filled three railroad cars. Then they were iced with 18 inches of crushed ice by using a conveyor blower with a four inch hose made of rubber and metal. The ice was crushed from 300 lb blocks of ice which were stored in the icehouse. Some of the sprouts were sent to freezers and were shipped in refrigerated trucks. This extra work consisted of loading grape sized boxes filled with sprouts and loaded 8 boxes high onto a hand truck and then went up a two feet high ramp to fill the truck. The ramp would get very wet and become slippery and dangerous, so we would wear rubber galoshes. It was actually like skiing. I developed a good knack at doing this and most of the drivers would request me to be their loader. It was hard work, but the pay was great. I got $5.00 for the single trailers and $8.00 for the double trailers. This extra money was great since I was trying to save money to buy a car. I was then asked if I would be interested in making the broccoli crates on the side and the pay was $.01 apiece. I said sure I'd like to try. I learned how to make them and got to the point that I could make one a minute. $.60 an hour was much better than $.35 an hour. I worked in a warehouse next to the bakery. There was a truck parked next to the warehouse that they used to haul the sprout barrels and it had high racks. I was getting very close to the age that I could drive and one day I found the key was left in the truck and I decided to give it a try. I practiced going back and forth for only about forty feet. One night while roaming around town I ran into Dwayne and Geronimo and we got the brilliant idea to take a ride in the barrel loaded truck. We went three miles up San Vicente Creek Road to the Quarry Camp.

We intended to turn around at the picnic ground but about 100 yards before that we ran into an overhead flume that carried spring water. The truck was too tall to make it under it so Dwayne and I tried to lift it, but we couldn't, and the flume came down and hit the truck cab putting a dent into it. We took the flume and laid it along side of the road and went on to the turn around. The truck was too long so we didn't have enough room to turn around. We backed up and ran into the oak trees causing some of the drums fall out. We picked up the ones that we could see, but it was too dark to really see them all and we were scared and just wanted to get the truck back. We got back thinking that we had gotten away with it. The next morning Jennie Wilson, who lived at the Quarry Camp, saw two drums up in the oak tree on her way to work at the Packing Shed and brought them with her. I still don't know how she got them out of the trees. It didn't take Curly long to figure it all out and took me with him to check out the truck. Then he took me to Mr. Poletti's office to tell him what we had done. He told me to give him the keys to the warehouse, that I would no longer be making the crates and that we would have to pay for fixing the flume. I was really lucky he let me go back to work. I'm sure that the only reason I didn't get fired was that they were really short of workers.

A group of us made a basketball hoop out of a pea hamper that we nailed up and we played during lunch break. Sometimes the guys that worked for the railroad that hauled the sprouts would get there around noon and would join us in the game.

The five women who sorted the Brussels sprouts were Adelina Brovia, Rose Steele, Incarnation Olimpio, Anita Demos and Ellena Moro. With the exception of Ellena there was, for some unknown reason, jealousy among the other women. They didn't get along at all. There was constant bickering and arguing and a few times actual fights would break out. It was a good thing that this was seasonal work. Because of the shortage workers they survived and didn't get fired, but Curly certainly had his hands full with them. I really found this rather comical.

During the busy season we processed the broccoli at night, 6:00

to 10:00 P.M. and Curly didn't work at night. Some of the guys who worked with me were Abby Novelli, Al Demos, George Vomvolakis and Fred Moro. There was also a man we called little Nick the Giant who was the Janitor, but he also worked with us. One evening we started a sprout throwing game, throwing the sprouts at each other. We knew that we had to clean up the mess so that we didn't catch hell. We cleaned up the inside, but we didn't realize that the doors were open during our fight and since it was dark none of us picked up on this. When Curly came to work the next morning there were sprouts all over the place and boy were we in trouble.

Another time George hit me with a piece of ice and started running away towards his house. I ran after him and when we got to the gate to his house his brother, Nick, was standing there and let George in and shut the gate. I hit it with a full head of steam and ended up really hurting myself and then on top of this Mrs. Vomvolakis came out gave me hell on top of it. I also got into an ice throwing incident with John Brovia. He had his back to me and when I threw a big piece of ice at him and hit him right in the back. Even though he was quite a bit older he started after me. I ran by the sprout barrels that were stacked really high and with quick thinking I kicked the lower barrel out and down they all came in front of him. I then went home and didn't even go back to work until the next day.

During our downtime we would play poker acting like real big shots. Our limit was a quarter and three raises. Even little Nick would play with us. Sometimes I would take salami from home and with a loaf of French bread we would have a feast, but we decided that to be real big shots we needed to have something to drink. Right across the street was the Ocean View Hotel and we were allowed to use their phone. I came up with the idea to ask to use the phone around 6:00 P.M. when they would all be in the dining room eating dinner. On the way to use the phone I could reach in and grab a bottle of whiskey and then go into the phone room. It had a door to outside and we would pass it to someone who waited there and then go back out of the phone room and out of the hotel. We never did this to get drunk, just to act like big shots and have fun with our feast. One time when we were playing the dealer called the game jacks or better and Abbie threw his cards in and said that he was never going to play that game again. When we asked him what he had in his hand he turned over 4 sevens!

Me and my classmates horsing around. I'm in the bottom row 2nd from right.

Richard Dietz's house when we were growing up.

*The first Davenport School House.
It became a home for the tramps and hobos of Davenport*

The Laguna Inn

Chapter Six

As I've already stated this was during World War II. An Army squadron rented the house next door to us where the Arvales family used to live. There were eight soldiers and a sergeant. Their duty was guard duty on the buffs behind the packing shed, not far from little shack that I ran away to. They were mainly looking for enemy ships. I became their mascot because I was alone so much of the time. They used to play a lot of poker until an argument broke out one day and the sergeant took the cards and tore them up. That was the end of poker. One night we had a terrible storm and at dawn a half dozen shots were fired by one of the guards on the bluffs. Then it was discovered that he was seeing one of the buoys that were used to help anchor the ships carrying cement bouncing around and the guard assumed we were being invaded. They were here for seven months.

The next group had four squads consisting of 32 men that were housed at the old Davenport Hospital across from the cement plant. They were a heavy artillery company and received permission from the Tambellini family to go onto their ranch onto a bluff overlooking the Pacific Ocean. They dug out enough dirt to hide two Howitzers and a look out post where they installed a high-powered scope to search for ships. As their mascot I enjoyed lots of pies, cakes and cookies made by the local families and given to the soldiers. Sergeant

Coulter took several of us on a tour inside the tunnels they had built in the bluffs. They went from low to high and high to low. This was to protect them from someone chasing them. This was pretty exciting to us. They ended up putting a cover of camouflage over it. We also got to look through the scope. I remember seeing Anno Nuevo Island about fifteen miles out. They used to use the Pacific School grounds for exercise. We even put a town softball team together to play against them on Saturdays. This did bring out a lot of the local people to cheer us on. The Tambelleni daughter, Nellie, ended up marrying one of the soldiers.

The next group to come was a really large Calvary company that headquartered at the Ferrari Ranch and a eucalyptus grove adjacent to the ranch. I assume that they were brought in out of concern of a possible Japanese attack. One of the soldiers, Frenchy Chavez started dating Fred Moros' sister, Yollie and he even came a few times on his horse. Fred and I were even able to ride the horse. This was pretty exciting stuff for us. I told Frenchy how much I like his Cavalry hat and he actually gave it to me. I liked it so much that I wore it until the brim finally fell apart.

During this same period The Davenport community set up an observation post with volunteers whose duty it was to document ships and plane travel. The first post was located on the second floor of the Ocean View Hotel and then a group built a two-story lookout tower in the empty field across from the Gregory's Country Store. Myrtle Garaventa was in charge of the two hour shifts of most of the town's people that were capable.

Chapter Seven

After graduating from Pacific Elementary I went to Mission Junior High and then to Santa Cruz High. We all rode the bus into Santa Cruz to school. The bus driver would leave Santa Cruz with a small bus and go to the San Mateo County Line and pick up kids all the way back along the Coast Highway to a garage next to the Cement Plant and pick up a larger bus. The Newtown kids caught the bus there and we caught it at the Davenport Cash Store around 7:00 A.M. We continued along The Coast Highway to Santa Cruz picking up kids at 10 to 12 ranches along the way and then stopped at Laurel Elementary then Mission Hill Junior High then the last stop was Santa Cruz High. We had two drivers who alternated Mr. Ross and Mr. Lear, Mr. Ross was also the wood shop teacher and Mr. Lear was the metal shop teacher at Mission Hill Junior High. A few times I missed the bus and was able to catch a ride with my neighbor, Josephine, and still get there on time. She wasn't a very good driver. On some of the curves she would sway off of the road, not so much as to wreck the car but enough to scare me. After a few times of this I didn't miss the bus anymore.

I really liked wood shop, math and gym and did well in these classes. The others I just managed to get by with mostly C's and D's.

We played softball all through grammar school constantly and high school and we became fairly good players. We decided to form a team – The Davenport Chokers. Richard, Fred, Eddie and Ted Cuclis and Louie DellaSantina were part of the team. Since we didn't have a manager when one of us made an error we would argue to the point that it could escalate into almost fist fights and a lot of bickering. This caused us to lose quite a few games. It had to be very comical for the fans to watch. Somehow Joe Vierra got wind of all of this and since he was a good player, he volunteered to be our manager. He turned the team around. We were playing in the C league and we went from last place to first place the following year. Then we were promoted to the Santa Cruz B league and we also joined a second B league in Felton. At this point we needed a sponsor so Don Dickson's father who was a member of the Optimist Club was able to get them to sponsor us. We had new red uniforms with white lettering. They were wonderful sponsors. They gave us the equipment we needed to complete the season and sponsored a dinner at the beginning of the season and one at the end of the season. We had a great season and won the B League title in both leagues. Don Dickson's Dad was so pleased and so proud that he got us a couple of more games, one in Dinuba against the All Stars which we lost. This was where his Dad came from. The other was in South San Francisco where we won. After the game we were taken to an Italian restaurant and then to a San Francisco Seals baseball game at Seals Stadium. We won both B league Championships the next year and then we went to Pescadero to play a double header and had a wonderful BBQ afterwards. We won both games.

We were so fortunate to have the Optimist Club as our sponsor. This made quite a difference in our growing up. We started with our school yards and that was our entertainment plus the radio show and maybe a dozen or so movies. Very few of us had bicycles, but some of us had wagons and a few BB guns. Everyone knows what kids have today. My message to parents today is to teach their kids that they need to earn their way by doing chores. They need to participate in the household and saving up for their desires. I started working at twelve years old and started buying my own clothes for school. It taught me that if I wanted something I worked for it and made me very proud to be able to do it for myself. It also taught me to save money for the future.

I woke up one morning really sick and wanted to tell Dad, but since I had cut school a few times and he found out I was afraid to tell him how sick I was. I waited until he left for work and then went back to bed. I had a fever all day and I was going in and out of consciousness. I kept looking at the clock thinking that a few hours had gone by and it was only fifteen minutes. When he finally got home and saw how sick I really was and said that he better take me to the Doctor. The Doctor told Dad to take me straight to the Hospital. They started giving me penicillin and Sulphur.

The priest came that evening to give me my last rites. I had strep throat and I really don't remember too much about all of this because of my condition. I do know that if I hadn't gone to the Hospital when I did, I probably wouldn't be writing this now.

Santa Cruz High didn't have a class in wood working so I decided to take Metal Shop which was a class my brother really excelled in. It didn't take long for me to figure out that this wasn't for me. I had a few confrontations with Mr. Brinkerhoff, the teacher, so one day he called me into his office. He told me that Tony was one of the best students he ever had and that I was the worst. I did give it my best and ended up with a D-grade and was really glad when it was over. He really wasn't very well liked by the whole class. He used to bring his lunch and a bottle of milk and set it on the podium. One day one of the better students, Gino Rossi, took his milk bottle and put it into the cooling barrel for the forge. When he noticed it was missing, he began asking us who took it. No one said a word. He made us sit at our desks for a half hour and kept asking over and over who took it. To this day I don't think he ever found out who did it.

I got by in my classes by looking over the shoulder of the girl sitting in front of me for three years. Then the moment of truth came. Graduation! I was five credits short. My counselor, Elva Miller, came to my rescue by arranging for me to file letters after school for Doc Fehlema's office. He communicated with a lot of Alumni who were in the Service during World War II and I filed the letters that he received from them. I will forever be thankful to Mrs. Miller for arranging this for me enabling me to graduate.

My biggest interest at this time of life was sports, after school football and baseball. My biggest hurdle was getting permission from Dad to allow me to participate. I went to our neighbor Mario Merlotti and asked him if he could help me with this by talking to my Dad about letting me try out for football. I asked him because he and my Dad would have a couple of glasses of wine and shoot the breeze once a week. Mario agreed to do it and a miracle occurred. He convinced Dad to reluctantly let me play. I went out for football and made the first team as a guard. Practice was over at 5:00 P.M. and if I got to Mission Street, two blocks away, before 5:30 I had a great chance of hitching a ride to Davenport. After 5:30 it was hit or miss catching a ride, but in my three years of sports I actually only had to walk home three times.

I had a great time playing football. On one occasion I was a little late to practice because of my letter filing. The coach used to put tape on the wall outside his office for us to use taping our ankles. There were two tapes left on the wall when I got to the gym and I when I grabbed them and headed to my locker. I heard someone say those are mine. I answered that I didn't see his name on them and proceeded to get dressed for practice. His name was Sweeney and was a senior and the team center. The seniors weren't too happy with me because I had beaten out the senior guard for the first string and it showed up sometimes by getting a little hectic at practice. After practice I took my shower and was getting dressed when my buddy, Eddie Root, alerted me that Sweeney was waiting for me outside the gym door. I walked through the door and then stepped back. He swung and hit the wall instead of me. I must admit that I beat the Hell out of him. I never had a problem with the seniors again, although I hitchhiked home with a bloody shirt from his nose.

Football was fun and actually good for me. Since we were short of players, we had to play both offense and defense. I don't remember what our record was, but I don't think that it was very good. I really liked Baseball better. I made first string center field my first year and by my third year I was playing several different positions. I was batting cleanup and doing great. We had a winning record although I really don't remember wins to losses.

I found that school dances and dating were far more important to me than studying. I didn't have a way to get there though. When I was a freshman in Hight School Al Demos would give me a ride. This worked out great. I would meet him at 11:00 P.M. at the corner of Mission Street and Younglove and he would take me home. This worked out fine until one time I lost track of time and didn't get there until 11:30. He called me a "sum of a bitch" and told me that if I was ever late again that he would go home without me. A month or so later I didn't get there until 11:15 and as promised he left without me. Scared as Hell I started walking slowly and praying for someone to come along and it was pretty cold. It wasn't until 2:30 A.M. that a bulk hauling cement truck and trailer went past me and then slammed on his brakes. The tires actually smoked. I ran up and opened the door and asked for a ride to Davenport. I got in and I got the joy ride of my life. I guess that the person who was scheduled to work that night didn't show up and so this guy got the call and was not at all happy about it. It was very fortunate that there was no other traffic because of the speed he was driving he was using both lanes. I was pretty darned scared. I asked him to let me off at the top of the hill. It was fast approaching so he came to a screeching halt and I got out I could smell the smoking tires. I caught Hell again from my Dad. I was never late for my ride again.

During the next couple of years rides became more available as Freddie and Abbie got their drivers licenses and had their own 4 door Model "A" Fords. We pooled moneys for gas which was fine with me since Dad wouldn't even consider the possibility of my getting my own driver's license. Now I could really go to the school dances and even make dates to go to the movies. It was a really fun time in my life. Then the parties at the Beach started. There were bon fires and beer drinking. There were occasional times when someone would have too much to drink, but there was always someone to lookout for them to see that they got home safely. We had a lot of fun when several of us guys would get together and have a harmonized sing-a-long. There were several places where we could buy beer and while we weren't angels and even though we partied no one ever had a car accident or got into drugs.

In this day and age there is quite a high percentage of high school and college kids doing drugs. They are risking the chance of changing their lives forever. My advice is to simply walk away and do not do drugs.

Chapter Eight

During my sophomore and junior years of High school I worked summers in the Brussels sprout ranches along the Coast Road from Santa Cruz to Davenport. I worked 10 hours a day 6 days a week at $.90 an hour. The planting was the hardest job of all. The plants were laid out two feet apart then planted into an 8" deep ditch with a hand hoe bending over from morning until noon and then picked plants the rest of the day. Some of the jobs consisted of irrigating row by row, cutting weeds from plant to plant and row by row and they had to be fertilized by hand. In between they had to be cultivated by a hand cultivator drawn by a horse. Next the crop had to be picked by hand rain or shine. I never had to do this.

One of the ranches I worked for grew a few acres of artichokes and the fertilizing was done by throwing a pitchfork full of chicken manure on each plant. I went with another farm worker to get the two horses harnessed up and hooked up to a wooden trailer and then went to the manure pile to load up the trailer. When I stuck my first pitchfork into the pile the odor was so bad that it almost knocked me out, but once I got used to it and it wasn't so bad. But I will never forget that first fork full and it was an experience that I will never forget.

I also worked for Leonard Domenichelli and I was cultivating a sprout patch near the ocean on a high cliff at the end of the row.

Leonard and Ted Cuclis came by in Leonard's Model "A" Ford. Leonard, joking, picks up a clod of dirt and threw it at Charlie, the horse and hits him in the rear. Charlie reared up, let out a fart and off we went. I tried sinking the cultivator deeper, but it didn't slow him down. We were zig zagging, knocking down plants and heading towards the bluff. I wasn't in any danger as all I had to do was to let go of the reins, but I was concerned about Charlie. I remembered something from horseback riding and grabbed one rein and proceeded to pull as hard as I could. I guess it hurt him and he reared up again and turned left and stopped not very far from the bluff. Leonard's joke almost ended in tragedy.

I also worked at the Ocean View Ranch and my boss's name was Noni. One afternoon he sent me to irrigate a sprout patch. It was hilly but I was doing fine. Mr. Noni came by and when he saw I was doing fine, without asking, he increased the volume of water in the rows and left to play cards at the hotel. This increased the water level in the ditches. As I got further down the patch there was a low spot just prior to the hilly section, I was supposed to put water in one ditch and turn it into the next ditch and hurry when the water went downhill. I had to put a check dam at each plant so that they got water. It's a good thing I was young because you only have so much time to hurry back and forth. By increasing the volume of water, the ditch broke at the low spot. I had to run to the end to do the check dams, run and fix the low spot and then run to turn the water into the next ditch. I kept this up for about an hour and a half thinking he would be back at any time to cut the volume down. He didn't and the water got away at the low spot. My tongue was hanging out and I got mad and was crying. I threw the shovel down the canyon, turned off the water and went home. I never worked for Mr. Noni again.

In my senior year some of my friends were working at a sawmill for Big Creek Lumber Co. The most exciting part of this was being paid $1.25 an hour for ten hours, six days a week. This was great so I applied and got the job. One of my coworkers, Moose Mitchell, was the tackle for the Santa Cruz High football team. Our duties were to pull the redwood lumber off the green chain and put it into lumber piles ready for shipping. This was located at the bottom of many canyons, so the working conditions were really hot. The green chain did not have rollers like the modern ones do so we had to drag each board. We made a pact that we weren't going to miss boards and let them go over the end. This was the hardest job that I ever had. We were both in really good shape, so we were able to do this difficult job. We never lost one stick of lumber over the end. Moose had to quit working two weeks prior to school starting, so the boss went to the unemployment office and hired men to replace him. By Saturday four of the men had quit and too many boards had gone over the end of the green chain.

I had another summer job at a ranch located right behind our house. I thought this was great because I could walk to work. I think it was my first test of what hard work was all about. I planted sprouts six days a week until 4:00 P.M. and then we would go pick the plants for the next day. My coworker was a Filipino named Nacara Deligdig. He only weight 120 pounds and I weighed 150 pounds. I had a really hard keeping up his pace, but I finally got to where I could keep up. The funniest part about all of this was our lunches; his consisted of two soup bowls held together with two rubber bands containing rice and two pieces of fish, like sardines, lying on top. My lunch was four sandwiches, a couple of pieces of fruit and a quart of party pack soda. Quite a difference in the two lunches.

During the winter I got a part time job on Friday nights at Caiocca's bakery from 6:00 P.M. to 2:00 or 3:00 A.M. making French bread. This was a really fun job and I got along well with the bakers so that after a few weeks they would have a pie they had baked for me. The pay was $.50 an hour. The reason there was such a large bake night on Fridays was because they did not bake on weekends.

Chapter Nine

After graduation I applied for work at the Telephone Company and P.G.&E. I could've gone back to work at a ranch or the Cement plant, but I really didn't want to do either. I was playing softball against my former coach and I explained to him that I had had no luck finding a job, so he asked me why I didn't put in my application at the cement Plant, something I really didn't want to do. After rethinking I did put in my application and got a job. I think with his possible help since he was a business agent for the union. I started my first job in the yard gang doing clean up in the yard areas, loaded and unloaded materials, etc. After six months I was sent to work with the plant carpenter Mario Giovanoni. He was working at this time on a new building which was to become a new office for the plant Mill Foreman. I started by digging the foundation trench. I didn't realize at the time that this was by first lucky break. We were framing and I loved it. After a few days Mario said that I was a good worker and I have an opening for a carpenter's helper and that he would request me if I wanted the job. I told him that I would be the best helper he ever had. They were updating and installing new equipment throughout the plant. We would get plans from the engineering department which showed the cement platforms and the bolt anchoring for each. We also repaired lots of wood stairs and railings. The wharf that extended a half mile out into the Pacific Ocean needed every spring one to two weeks of deck and railing repairs. When I worked there, I would bring my coffee can fishing equipment and do a little fishing while I worked. Whenever I caught one, I would mark the spot for future fishing. Another place I liked to work was the quarry where we went into the tunnel and built new loading platforms. We also did a lot of galvanized metal exterior walls and roof repairs. The third week on the job the yard boss, Mr. Shaw, took me to a job to dig a ditch for a water line about 150 feet long and one foot wide and fifteen inches deep. He told me that they were going to install the water line the next day. My first thought was that there was no way I could get this done, but with the shortage of jobs I realized I had better get it done. There was a cement crust 2" thick and I had to use a pick to break through. I went 10 feet at a time and actually got it done by quitting time and still had a job.

One project that almost ended my working at the cement plant occurred after I had been there two years. We were sent to the kiln room area to put in a cement wall ten feet high in place of the corrugated metal wall. This meant several of the kilns had to be shut down. The company was in a hurry to get them restarted, but before they could be we had to install one row of corrugated siding to finish. The day we were scheduled for the job it began to rain and the wind was blowing very hard making the work very dangerous. I was on the outside of the building hanging onto a rope scaffold. It was moving with the wind and the rain made it slippery. I had on rain gear, but when I bent over the water would run down my back. I struggled, but we got about four sheets on. My job was to punch holes and install wire tie anchors. Mario's job was to hold the sheet firm while I did this and to fasten the ties. Because of the rain this was becoming more and more dangerous. We thought that we should take a break and wait until the rain stopped. Mario talked to our boss about our waiting out the rain and he said that we needed to get it done, so we kept on going. At the fifth sheet a big gush of wind came up and Mario let the sheet move and I missed the punch and took a direct hit on my thumb. I lost my temper and threw the hammer about 50 yards. I told Mario I was done. He agreed. On the way back to the shop I stopped at the office for first aid where they made a hole in my nail which did give me some relief. I finally got to the shop, I was supposed to rip some boards on the table saw, I tipped the table, loosened the saw rocker arm and it stuck. I gave it a good jerk and broke the cast iron rocker arm. I looked out the window and saw Mr. Kinzie, the plant superintendent, coming. He came into the shop and said I have two men who don't want to install the metal siding. Since we didn't answer he said it again. I waited for Mario to say something since he was my boss.

Finally, I showed him my thumb, explained what happened and told him how dangerous it was. I explained to him that when the rain stopped it could be done in four hours and no one would get hurt. It was just too dangerous to do it now and if he didn't think so then he should go try it. No one said a word. I assumed I was fired, grabbed my lunch and started to leave. I said I was looking for a job when I got this one. The next thing I know Mario grabbed his lunch started to leave too. Mr. Kinzie said for us to just wait a minute that we were probably right and that we should wait until the rain stops. I still think if Mario had not made the move, I would have lost my job. It stopped raining after lunch, and the wall was completed by quitting time.

One day, a couple of months later, I was asked if I would be willing to do metal roof replacements. Mario couldn't do it because he had fallen off a roof before and was afraid of heights. I was briefed by the plant engineer, Danny Falcone and was given five laborers to work with. The first roof was probably the biggest roof, about 35 feet high and over the kilns. We worked on a rolling scaffold that worked off the roof beams. We used all types of ropes and planks and started to tear off the old roof a section at a time. We installed the new roof at this section in the morning and then in the afternoon would tear off another section. We used this method to work around the afternoon winds. I admit it was scary, but at age 22 it was pretty exciting too. This went so well they gave us a second roof on a building called the Raw Mill. I look back now I realize we saved the company a lot of money. After we completed this I had a surprise visit from Mr. Kinzie. He offered me a job to run a D-6 cat and a clam shell shovel moving raw materials to make the cement. I really didn't want to give up my carpenter job so I asked him if I could think about it. It meant I would be the relief equipment operator and it meant swing and graveyard shifts every other weekend. My first thought was to just say no, but I knew that this would go over very well. I came up with the idea to try it for two months, but if I didn't like it, I could return to my job in the carpenter shop. He agreed. I did my two months and then notified the yard boss that I preferred working in the carpenter shop and per the agreement I returned to my job until May of 1953 when I got drafted.

1948 Me and one of my High School buddies.

Chapter Ten

After High School I played softball with several different teams. I was asked first to play with the Swiss Dairy team, the local semi pro baseball team. It was also at this time that the young lady I had been dating since high school became pregnant. We sat down with her parents and discussed the situation and they told us it was up to us. I was 20 and Charlotte was 18 when we got married. Now I was going to have a complete family of my own and I was pretty damned excited about it. My job at the cement plant was going well so after six months we were able to purchase our first home and furniture. The house was only 800 sq feet, but it had two bedrooms, one bath, a nice little kitchen and a nice little living room. We put in a front sidewalk to the street and added a cement patio at the rear. January 17, 1951 Joe Jr. was born healthy and well. I was so excited. Things were really going well, until six months later when our marriage became very rocky for various reasons including our young ages. We only made it for another year when we separated and then divorced. We did try several times to get back together, but Charlotte had started dating other men in the interim and it just didn't work. She wanted $500.00 to take her name off the house so I found a way to get a loan and was able to pay her and keep the house. The worst part was that my son, Joe Jr. was gone. The next few months were a fog. I worked my five days a week, but on weekends I would go to the Asti Bar and do some heavy drinking and on Sundays sober up to be ready for work on Mondays.

Because of all of this my draft status changed and five months later I got the draft notice from the Army and was off to Fort Ord. For the next 16 weeks I trained in a heavy weapons company. Up at 4:30 every morning and then an hour and a half march to the different range locations. The discipline was very strict and if anyone messed up you could end up at the end of the day cleaning pots at the mess hall or cleaning weapons at the weapons pool for a couple hours. Actually, a lot of our youth in this day and age could use this type of discipline then maybe it could result in a better country for all of us. Once when we were lining up for dress parade and no one was supposed to move I slightly moved my head and was called to front and center and ordered to go up the steps to the landing where the Company Commander put me at attention for an hour until they got back from the parade field. I learned a good lesson.

The next two weeks we were at Camp Hunter Legget for bivouac living in tents for two men and eating C rations, training in desert like conditions. After the bivouac we had to march 26 miles. We really dreaded this, but we did it even though several guys did pass out.

Then it was back to Fort Ord and the following week we received orders for Korea. We spent the next week with a duffle bag and getting our cloth issue. Suddenly the war over and everything came to a halt. The next morning during roll call, a list of 53 names was read and when we were assembled and were asked if we would be interested in going to leadership school for eight weeks with the opportunity of receiving a promotion to PFC. I agreed and started another eight weeks of training. We had to march double time to every class and wore ties. After I finished the eight weeks of additional training Rank was frozen, so I not only did not get a PFC stripe I didn't get the extra money that would have come with it.

My next orders were to report to North Front at Fort Lewis, Washington to a company that installed metal bridges. This meant working outside in the rain every day. After the fourth week of this the First Sergeant asked for a volunteer who could type. I raised my hand so fast that my arm almost came out of the socket. He asked about my typing and I told him I had taken one semester of typing at school and that I wasn't fast, but pretty accurate. He told me he was sending me to Main Fort where I would have four hours a day typing and four hours of administration. After the eight weeks I came back as our company clerk. I was out of the rain and no more K.P. or guard duty.

When I arrived at Fort Lewis, I found out that our company's pay records were lost and that I would only receive 15% of my pay. Writing home and asking for money was not an option. I asked around about a loan from anyone and was told that I could borrow, but the pay back was 5 for 10. In other words, when borrowed $5.00 I would have to pay back $10.00 on payday therefore I borrowed very little. When I finally received my three months back pay the other clerk and I decided to start a loan lending partnership. This worked out great since I worked in the orderly room and I had access to our company pay roster. We used that as a guide as to how much we would lend. On Payday we made sure we collected the money and this extra money really helped. I got to go to town on weekends and had a much better time than I could have had on just my Army pay.

I stayed at Fort Lewis for another year and received orders to report to back to Hunter Leggett where I lived in a squad tent that had wood floors and a pot belly stove that burned coal. Our mission was to prepare an existing road and to install several metal bridges over creeks. The road extended from Hunter Leggett to San Simeon at the Hearst Castle property. The army had worked out an exchange with the Hearst family that we would install the road and the bridges then they would allow the Army an amphibious landing area at San Simeon Beach. The tanks were moved in, proceeded up the hill past the castle to a big open meadow. Since no one had checked out the property they did not know that the soil was quicksand type. Three tanks sunk to a standstill and they brought in a crane that also sunk and then a large cat. The whole maneuver was canceled. A lot of that equipment ended up being stolen.

Two weeks later I was transferred back to the processing center at Fort Or. And two weeks later I was discharged. Just prior to my discharge I was offered Sergeant Status and that I would be the Company first sergeant. I told my company commander that I would consider it, but I really had no intention of re-upping. I will say that my experience in the army was good. It was not only good discipline it took me away from my problems in Santa Cruz and it gave me a chance to think out what I wanted to do with the rest of my life.

Chapter Eleven

I went back home to live with my Dad and my new stepmother, Carolina because I needed to save money. My Dad and I had worked out our problems and things were much better between us. I went back to work at the cement plaint with the intention of working there for about six months to save some money and to try to get into the Carpenters Union. I wanted to get out of maintenance work and become a full-fledged carpenter. Mario, by boss, had back surgery and ended up out of work for six to eight months. They hired another carpenter and made him the head carpenter which kept me at helper status. Before, when Mario went on vacation, I was appointed the head carpenter, so I went to the business agent, Joe Vierra and complained that I thought that with Mario gone I should be the head carpenter and should not have lost my seniority by being in the service. He had a meeting with Mr. Kinzie and was successful in getting me the head carpenter's position. The new head carpenter became upset and quit. I never thought Mr. Kinzie was happy about giving me the head carpenters position because the first week he made a point of coming to the carpenter shop to tell me I would be doing jobs that required me to follow blueprints. I told him that I had done this before I went into the Army and I didn't see a problem. One of my first jobs was to set 10 pair of concrete piers as anchors to support steel posts for the new conveyor system.

The conveyor system installers came and checked everything out and found that it was perfect. There were several more projects of supports and anchoring new equipment with no problems. Rumors had it that I was really doing them a good job and doing them a favor by staying until Mario came back to work. I was told by the plant engineer that I was doing an excellent job. I was given a job building a 20 x 24 sewing room that was to be used for fixing dust collector socks. It was being built inside of an existing large warehouse. My helper Ralph Leaf was 65 years of age and wore bifocals. We framed the walls and put on the roof rafters and then we were supposed to put the roof sheathing on the overhang. I wanted to lay four or five rows of roof sheathing creating a platform to walk on. I didn't want Ralph on the roof until this was completed. I told him to bring over roof sheathing and other materials to keep him busy until I completed the walk. Ralph had kept busy packing boards. When he had finished the job, he was just standing there watching me. I noticed the superintendent standing at the warehouse door and he saw Ralph standing idle. The timing was terrible; it presented the completely wrong picture. The superintendent sent my boss to tell me that I had someone just standing around idle and that this was unacceptable. I tried to explain to him about why I had done it this way and that I didn't understand why Mr. Kinzie didn't come to talk to me himself. I told him that I would go and find Mr. Kinzie and take care of this myself. After about 20 minutes I found him in the yard foreman's office. I waited until he came out and we walked towards his office while I tried to explain why I did the job the way I did. I told him how upset I was about his being constantly on my case when I was only staying on the job to help them until Mario got back to work and that I was going to pick up my tools at the carpenter shop and leave. He turned red and didn't say another word. I got my tools and loaded them in my car. I stopped by the office and asked for a check and they told me to come back the next day at 4:00. I did and they didn't have it ready and assured me that they would have it the next day. I went back and it was ready. Mr. Macauley told me that Mr. Kinzie was in his office and would I care to go and talk to him. My answer was no that I had said all I had to say the day I quit. I will say that looking back on my early life and the way I was teased that maybe I was too sensitive. I will always be thankful for the opportunity that I got there to learn and get started in carpentry.

For years afterwards when I attended High School Reunions and I was asked what college I went to I always said Davenport City College, referring to the Cement Plant.

After leaving the Plant Mario put me in contact with the Carpenters Union business agent, Sam Combs. I went for an appointment and he asked me how long I had worked at the Plant and I told him four years. He said that four years are required to be a journey man carpenter and that he could sign me up as a journey man. I told him that my experience was limited so he suggested that they could credit me two years and complete the next two years in the apprentice program. I liked that because I could ask questions and not worry about being fired. He called me a few days later and said that he had an opening in heavy construction putting pillar supports in for the River Street Bridge. I went to River Street and worked there for two months when the rains came. The water rose up and the job shut down for the winter. I went to pick up my check and the superintendent Ken Foote called me into his office to tell me that he was pleased with effort and wanted to know if I was interested in working for Bogard Construction who was building custom homes in the West Lake area. I was very excited and told him yes, I was interested. He said he would call them and put in a good word for me. I thanked him and left very excited.

I happened to run into Pete Pianavilla that same evening. He asked me if I knew Paul Hirsch, a general contractor who lived in Davenport. He said that Paul was looking for a carpenter and that he would take me to his house to meet him. I told him that I was still an apprentice not a journeyman and he said it wouldn't hurt to meet him. We went to Paul's house and we talked. During the conversation Pete vouched for me and told Paul that he knew that I'd be a good worker. Paul said that he would think about it overnight and would let me know in the morning. Now I was really confused.

JOEY

Which way do I go? I decided to ask my Dad for his opinion and after a while he suggested that if it were him, he would go to work for Paul because he was a small contractor and that I would learn more from him. Well, I really went to bed confused. I was leaning toward Bogards. By morning I had decided to first wait for Paul and if he didn't come, I would go to Bogards and apply. Well Paul did come and said that he would like for me to come to work for him. As I write this now, I'd have to say it was a very lucky break. We got along very well, and I knew that I had found what I really wanted to do. He was a very hard worker and a great boss.

My training was working very hard and asking questions and going to apprenticeship school and putting it all together. I then started taking the building plans home and tried to visualize what I would be doing the next day. After a short time, I could see that this was really helping me learn. Next, we were working on the roof and I packed the lumber and he cut the entire roof on the ground and then we both went up and installed it and everything fit perfectly. I was so impressed that I started thinking about learning how to cut a complete roof myself. I decided to build a doghouse for our dog. I built a doghouse with two rooms, because by doing it this way I would have to cut a hip and valley rafter which is harder to do than common rafters. I did it and it looked great. I couldn't wait to try and cut a real roof by myself.

The next step was installing the cabinets, doors and trims and hardware. I was getting more excited every day.

Then we started a new house. I had my first experience with foundations and the laying out the house and the footings. At this time the footings were done with a pick and shovel and this was really hard work, but still exciting. We were also working on a garage next to a custom building for none other than my friend Pete Pianavilla. I got to cut my first roof and Paul came to help me install it. It fit perfectly.

We continued building more houses together and I kept learning not only from on -the -job training but also by going to apprentice school. On my own I started taking more plans home and taught myself how to read them. This not only helped me see what we were doing on a day -to -day basis it helped learn faster and showed Paul that I was really interested in learning.

We used to pour cement from wheelbarrows and now they have concrete pumpers which allow you to pour anywhere. Now nailing guns have taken the place of the most tedious of jobs nailing by hand. Next came aluminum and vinyl windows to replace the packaged wood windows and frames that we had to put together. Pre-hung doors have taken the place of hanging doors and trims from scratch. And lastly roofs now come in a complete truss package. The old ways taught me to actually work on any kind of construction and the new ways taught me there was an easier way.

Our work increased and Paul gave me a house to frame with another carpenter he had hired and put me in charge. I was so elated and there was no way I was going to let him down and I didn't. We got the house done with no problems.

Around this time paneling had become very popular so I became the paneling specialist. Most houses then had a room or two of paneling. This really helped me out during the rainy season. I had very little lost time.

Some of the things that helped us were that on occasion we would work on Saturdays to keep us on schedule. I never turned in my time and if I was on a job that would only take me an hour to finish I did so on my own time so that this freed me up for Paul to send me to a new job the next day saving him time and money.

Paul and his wife, Betty, bought a couple of acres in Bonny Doon to build themselves a new house on. Then Paul bought a house which was the caretakers house located at the Swanton Fish Hatchery for a very reasonable price. Paul wanted to salvage the lumber from this house to be used on their new home. I volunteered to help him out and it took us four weekends to complete the salvage work. Then we started the new house. There was enough lumber for everything but the garage framing, the roof and exterior siding. This was a company job, but I did work a few Saturdays free gratis. Betty found a picture of a living room wall similar to theirs with a fireplace and window on each side and the paneling was done in checkerboard pattern. Paul was complaining about the cost to do this. I thought about this overnight and went to work the next day and told him that since Betty had been so nice to me by sending me pie several times a week that if he bought the paneling and cement then I would do it for her on weekends for nothing. Betty got her checkerboard paneling, so everyone was very happy with how well it turned out.

We were nearing completion on a beautiful custom home next door to Paul's house when Paul told me while we were having lunch that he was losing money on the job. I asked him why and he explained that he had not included the air conditioning or electrical bids when he totaled so he was running out of money for the completion. I was doing the finish work and had only the family room to finish with cherry wood paneling and an entertainment center with cherry panel doors so I told him that I would do it for free the next two weekends. I never asked how the end cost came out, but I know he appreciated what I had done and thanked me for it.

One day when I was picking up materials at Santa Cruz Lumber Roy Johnson asked If I would be interested in doing some small jobs for some of their customers. Like hanging doors, repairing windows etc. I told him that I would run it by Paul and get back to him. I asked Paul he said to go right ahead and do them since those were the kind of jobs that he couldn't make any money on. I went back and told Roy yes. They started giving me job and it worked out very well. This not only helped me out financially it also gave me the opportunity to gain quite a bit of experience. I owed Paul thanks for letting me do these jobs.

Partly because of Paul and Betty's new home in Bonny Doon, new construction escalated in this area and the workload grew larger and he hired more carpenters. I was actually put in charge of some jobs and I was so pleased and loving the responsibility, I actually went to the job each day thinking about how I could help Paul make money. If a roof needed bracing I would do it myself because I could do it faster. I was so happy I could hardly wait for the next day to see how much I could get done. One of the homes was for a

Mr. Larsen and the exterior siding was clear 1 x 10 redwood bevel siding and the o.s. corners were mitered which meant no trim. I was really thrilled doing this job; I got there early and often stayed late. At lunch I would watch the deer and the quail. Talk about peace and quiet. What made it even better was the thank you I got from the owner telling me what a great job I had done.

The house on Alta where Charlotte and Joe Jr. and I lived.

Chapter Twelve

After my divorce, from Charlotte, I would pick up Joe Jr. a couple of times a month in Los Gatos for the weekend. On one of these weekends on my way back home I stopped at the Acacia Inn on Highway 17 and met Loraine Cohen there. We dated for a year or so and while I was really fond of her, I was concerned because she had two children and I wasn't sure I was ready to take on this responsibility. I started thinking about how she kept her home, took care of her children and all the nice things that she did for me. I realized that I really did love her and asked her to marry me. I didn't know it then, but this was one of the luckiest days of my life when she said yes. We were married in Santa Cruz and I moved into her home on Ocean View Avenue. I started my new life with Loraine and two children to raise, child support to pay, house payments to make and about $600.00 in the bank. We both worked. I was working for Paul and Loraine was working for the Telephone Company. There were many adjustments to make and believe me I needed a lot of adjusting. I soon learned how much I was loved and for the first time in my life I felt that I had found someone who really understood me. I found a part of life that I had missed all of my life. We had great communication. After we got home from work, we would sit down, have a cup of coffee and talk about work, the kids and all the things that needed our attention. We would agree on solutions and stick with them. At times I would come home grumpy and nasty and all I would get from her was love and kindness. She did such a good job that I would go to work the day thinking about what a big ass I had been. I was so lucky to find my Loraine. At the end of our first year of marriage we had our first child, Michael. At this point Loraine quit working and stayed home to raise the three kids. Finances were tight, raising three kids and paying the child support made it tough. I can remember buying shoes for the kids – one would get new shoes on one paycheck and one would get them the following paycheck. There were many time friends would ask us to go out to dinner with them and we would have to refuse because we just couldn't afford it. In order to get ahead I talked to Santa Cruz Lumber about increasing my weekend jobs and they obliged. With my ambition and hard work and Loraine's ability to save money everything started to go well. By our fourth year our second child, Jo Ann, was born. Now, Loraine did a really wonderful job raising this mob.

We joined the Surf Twirlers square dancing club and went every Wednesday night and occasionally go to hoe downs at different locations. We still picked up Joe Jr. every two weeks and sometimes he would bring three or four of his friends with their sleeping bags and their surf boards. Loraine would load them and their surfboards into our station wagon and off they would go. We had Little League, Boy Scouts and Girls Scouts and then my years with the Seahawks when I had my very own rooting section. My work averaged six to seven days a week and occasionally Loraine would complain about the time I spent working and that we weren't taking any family vacations. I ignored her. I took it the wrong way until the next day while eating lunch I thought it over and realized that she was right. I went home that evening and told her that I would only work every other weekend and yes, we needed a vacation and I needed to spend more time with my family. I was concerned though because we were saving money and getting ahead, but her answer to me was you might end up with a lot of money, but you won't have a family to share it with.

We got together with my buddies Richard, Fred and Eddie and

their wives. We usually got together a couple of times a year with our kids for barbecues and games. Richard said that he had gone to Bucks Lake on a camping vacation with his family when they found out about a lottery for 48 lots with a lease for 99 years renewable every 20 years. We jokingly decided to put in one name, but it would include all four families. To our great surprise we got one of the lots. We four guys got together to decide about ownership and to decide the type of vacation cabin to build. We did know that four families could not have joint ownership, so we agreed that Richard would be listed as the owner and would handle all of the dealings. By hand shake the four of us agreed that each family would hold 25% ownership – this was in 1962 and a couple of years ago we jointly agreed to sell it.

We decided to build an A frame cabin. On a Friday after work the four of us went to Bucks Lake with our sleeping bags. We got there after dark and couldn't find our lot so we found an open meadow and brought out our sleeping bags and even though it was a bit scary went to sleep. Next day we found our lot and agreed that we got a nice deal. I drew the plans as needed for the building permit and made the material list. We filed for the permit and got it approved. I talked to Paul about a vacation combined with the 4th of July holiday to give us 10 days. The lumber was ordered to be delivered the first week of July. We loaded up all the tools plus the nails and off we went. We worked for the next 10 days from daylight to dark. We completed the exterior siding, roof and the bracing of the roof for the snow load. The three of them worked really hard through blisters and all and never complained. I had a wonderful surprise while we were there, Loraine took a Greyhound Bus and came up for Saturday and Sunday. What a surprise – she was always doing nice things for me. I know that's why I was so happy and successful.

We put the plans in motion for finishing the cabin the following year. This way I was able accumulate the items that were needed to complete the work. I was able to acquire the interior and exterior wood doors, cabinets for the kitchen, a freestanding electric stove. We completed a bedroom, bathroom and kitchen downstairs, a bedroom and open mezzanine upstairs, V.A. tile throughout, the painting, septic tank and a water system from an existing spring that served other cabins as well. Every year we drew a number one through four, with number one having the preferred time at the cabin. All of our families enjoyed vacations there for the next forty years.

Chapter Thirteen

Into the ninth year of working with Paul I began to get itchy about getting my own contractor's license and going into business for myself. I discussed it with Loraine and explained to her that I owned most of the tools that I needed and that if I could run the work that I had for Paul I would be able to do it for us. She said that it was up to me. I started studying and getting ready to take the test. I told Paul what I was doing. He offered to give me a reference letter which I needed since I needed three reference letters. I took the test and passed. I quit my job thinking that I could get started right away. I called in a couple of days to find out where my license was and was told that it takes six weeks to arrive. I was too embarrassed to go back to Paul. I went to the Union Hall and signed up on the list. I told them I only wanted to work on custom homes.

Within two days I got a call to go to Aptos and was hired. I explained that it would only be until I got my license and the boss said that was fine. I installed a dumb waiter and then installed the paneling in a building that had four condos. In the 5th week I told him I could work only until I got my first job. Santa Cruz Lumber referred me to see a Mr. Larson on Trout Gulch Road in Aptos. He wanted to put a foundation under an old house, new windows, new siding, roof etc. I was about to tell him that it might be better to tear it down when he said that he was born in the house and this was the way he wanted to do it. He also said that he wanted to work with the contractor that he hired. I told him that was fine with me and that I wanted to work ten hour a day six days a week for $.25 over scale and a 3% profit. I told him I would give him an hour's work for an hour's pay and anytime he was unhappy we could cut it back. He thought about it and said o.k. and that I had been given a good recommendation from the lumber yard. He decided that he also wanted a a barn. The whole job took six months to complete. He was happy and so was I. I really needed the money.

Next the Lumber Yard sent me to Dottie and John Gray in Pleasure Point on Rock View Drive. They gave me a job to build a carport. This job was in a residential area and the other one was out in the country which meant I could only work five days a week. Before I was finished with the job Dottie said that she wanted a new kitchen. I got some pictures of kitchens and went to work. Then she wanted cabinets built on the living room fireplace wall, and then new windows throughout the house and then finally a roof extension and a glass room looking out on the ocean.

I ran into Paul at the Lumber Yard and we chit chatted about work and how busy we both were. He asked if I had to time to have a cup of coffee and so we went. He said that he had been thinking about how well we got along and how well we worked together and wanted to know what I thought about forming a partnership. I really liked the idea. He agreed that there would no buy in required since I had helped build the company. I also told him that I agreed with him about our working well together except for the P.R. part. We had had an experience on a nice home when the wife decided that they wanted to make some changes in the master bath vanity. I told them I would call Paul and set up an appointment for 9:00 the next morning to go over the changes. The next day they showed up at 9:00 but he didn't. They were upset and I was really embarrassed. I told them that I would set it up for the same time the next day. They said o.k., but I could tell they were not happy. It upset my whole day. I called him that night and told him that if he didn't show up that I would load up my tools and go to the union hall and look for another job. He showed up this time. I reminded him about this so he agreed that I should run the P.R. part and that he would run the work. I said o.k., but I needed to talk to Lorraine first and that I would get back to him. She again said that whatever I decided to do was fine with her. I wanted to make sure that we were on the same page. We met for lunch and went over everything. We discussed tools, equipment, duties, money etc. and it turned out we were both pretty much on the same page. We hired an attorney that we both knew to write up the partnership agreement and our company became Hirsch & Aliberti General Contractors.

We started with $5,000.00 each that we put into an account. I suggested to Paul that we should just leave the original investment in the account and take the same salary as the carpenters. We agreed and continued taking only a carpenter's salary the next year and took only 50% of the total profit. By doing it this way we would be financially able to expand our company if we wanted to.

I set my first office up in our dining room then moved to our master bedroom and finally ended up in our garage with a partial office and material storage. Paul was handling the construction work foundation through completion of the exterior. My duties were bidding and ordering and then working on the finishing end of the jobs. I scheduled the subcontractors and worked with the homeowners. We started getting requests for custom remodeling and actually had a pretty good first year. The second year I actually bid a little more work than we could handle so Paul and I worked quite a few Saturdays and even a few Sundays in order to keep up with the work and keep the customers happy. This was great during the good weather months, but the winter months (December to March) we had to struggle to keep everyone working due to the rain. We were lucky to break even. Luckily, I ran into an old friend who was an adjuster for an insurance company. He wanted us to bid repairs and replacements for a fire job. I asked him to send us the breakdown and then I submitted our bid. We got the job, completed it and everyone was happy. A couple of weeks later we got a call about a major fire caused by Christmas tree lights. I submitted the bid, got the job, and completed it and the Adjuster and the owner were both pleased. Then he introduced us to other adjusters which lead to more winter work and we ended up making a profit.

We were developing growing pains and decided to rent a place where we could set up our table saw and store our miscellaneous tools. Two weeks later as I was returning from a job up the coast I got to the West side and saw a MLS sign on a metal building on the corner of Swift and McPherson Street. I went down the street to Al Medina's real estate office (which we had built) and asked him about the building. He told me that it had been on the market for about three years, and he thought that we could get it for a good deal. He called me the next day and told me that we could buy it for $27,500.00 and I said yes. That evening I called Paul and told him. I also told him that it was a truck dock building four feet off of the ground with three rollup doors and an office area and that in order to get the pickups in and out that we could just build a ramp at the end door. So, now we have an official office and shop to work out of. We paid cash so we had no payments and best of all no rent payments. We had the winter insurance work and could not have been more pleased with our business.

Paul and I were working on a job up the coast where we could see Anno Nuevo Island a mile off the coast. We were eating lunch Paul said he had a boat and that the fishing was probably great out there. We decided to try it on Saturday and met in Davenport. Paul also brought his neighbor Mr. Mertha who was a double amputee, both legs at the knees, and we all loaded into the boat. Paul said that the waves looked great for getting to the island. I was sitting in the front, Mertha was in the middle and Paul was in the rear doing the steering. We got 300 yards from the island and I yelled to Paul that the waves were getting much bigger now. I told him there's one coming from each side and take his pick. Then they met right in front of the boat and we got about 9 inches of water in the boat. Then the motor quit running, so we were drifting back toward shore. Paul was trying to get the engine restarted and Mertha and I were bailing water with coffee cans. We drifted for a good half hour.

When we were 500 yards from shore Paul finally got it restarted and then asked us if we should try again and we both answered NO let's go back to shore and go home. That was the end of my first fishing trip, safe and sound.

    The second trip Paul and I went to the Delta in Antioch to fish for striped bass. He had a fourteen feet boat. I was really excited since I had never been striper fishing before. It was 9:00 in the morning and there were quite a few boats out that were quite a bit larger than ours. We looked like a dingy. We were ready to set the anchor when Paul realized that he had brought the kelp anchor instead of the sand anchor that we needed. He decided to hook the kelp anchor to a marking buoy which you were never supposed to do. It worked and we started fishing. We were out three to four hours and no fish when the wind came up and the white caps became bigger and stronger and most of the other boats had left. We were so eager to catch a striper we stayed a little longer. By now we were getting quite large swells and we decided that we better get the Hell out of there. Because of the conditions it took us a good fifteen minutes just to get the anchor off of the buoy. I was helping to guide us between swells all the while thinking just get me back to the dock. This was the second time, and believe me, there was never going to be a third fishing trip.

    In my travels around Santa Cruz with our various jobs I kept hearing about UCSC building a campus in Santa Cruz and that there was going to be a need for apartment housing. I thought that with our reserve fund it might be a wise investment for us. Paul and I met for a Saturday lunch to discuss the potential for our company. I suggested to him that we call Al Medina, realtor, to locate possible sites for apartments. We could do the building plans and would have no trouble obtaining a building loan using our reserve account as collateral. He was very surprised to find out that we had $185,000.00 in this account. He said he wanted the weekend to think about it and that he would get back to me on Monday. He came in on Monday and we went into my office. He said that while my ideas were very good, he really wasn't interested. He had always wanted to invest in a cattle ranch. This really upset me. I knew how great it could have been for both of us. Two weeks later he came into my office and after much hemming and hawing proceeded to tell me that he had purchased a cattle ranch in Oregon. After thirteen years of working together I didn't want to say something wrong, so I just said that we'd talk about it later because I was livid. After a while he came in and told me about his intentions. He wanted to leave July 1st and suggested that we hire a carpenter to replace him and maintain our partnership. My bubble was completely burst. I needed to do some serious thinking. We had a no goodwill clause in our partnership agreement which meant that neither partner had to buy the others interest in the business. I wanted to continue on with the business with no interruption, so after a lot of thinking I finely came up the plan that helped us part as friends. My Plan was that the partnership would continue until September 30th and any contracts signed after this date would be my personal contracts. Even though he would be leaving early he would still receive wages, and his share of the profits on our joint contracts. We would have the Swift Street property appraised and he would get half of the increase in value which was about $16,000. I thought this was fair for both of us as it would leave me able to continue on without interruption. He accepted this and we made an appointment with the attorney and had the proposal made official. The first of July Paul left for his ranch in Oregon and the name was changed to Joe Aliberti Construction Inc. on October 1st. All contacts were completed by Dec 31 and the monies were disbursed as agreed and we went our separate ways.

Chapter Fourteen

As the kids were growing up the house seemed to be getting smaller and it became crowded. We had only one bathroom. So, we decided to remodel by adding a bedroom, bathroom and redoing the kitchen. We updated the plumbing and electrical and removed the wallpaper, textured and painted room by room. Took some time because we did it on weekends and it was really hard work, but it was really worth it.

We also started to think about investments. We started with stocks and soon realized that we knew nothing about stocks and decided to turn to real estate. We purchased a complex of four three-bedroom apartments on 34th Avenue and then a four-unit apartment complex on Blackburn. So now we became landlords. Loraine took charge of renting the units I was in charge of the repairs. After a year or so we began discussing the possibility of building a new home and started looking for a lot. We found and bought two lots on Western Drive on the West side. Not long after we bought them UCSC was built so Western Drive became a main thoroughfare and we didn't want to build or raise our kids there. Our investment sat there. We continued looking and a really nice lot became available on Prospect Heights on the east side. A house could be built with an Ocean View, but we weren't really ready to build yet so since it was such a good buy we went ahead and purchased it. With this purchase our reserves were getting low so our investing came to a temporary halt.

I was then asked to bid a fire damage on a dwelling in Scotts Valley that sits on an acre with an acre parcel next to it. It came on the market as a complete package and the location is a mile from Highway 17 and is in a separate valley with great views on a private road. The owner was a partner of Santa Cruz Construction which had filed bankruptcy after building several homes and he moved away. The house was rented briefly but it was mostly vacant. It was vacant when the fire occurred and it was determined that it was an arson fire, but they were never able to prove it and the owner was paid off by the insurance company for the cost of the repairs. The original sale price was "as is burnt" and included the adjoining acre $16,500.00. Six months later I got a call to go check out a water damage in Scotts Valley. I decided to take the folder with the estimate that I had prepared on the fire damage with me. After I finished the estimate for the water repairs, I went back to take a second look at the fire damaged house. I drove to the empty lot next door and went up the hill behind the house so that I could look down on it. I could see all the changes that could be made and the improvements that I could make. The location was great as well as the view – I became really excited and couldn't wait to get home to discuss the possibility of our buying it with Loraine. I suggested that we should buy it and I could rebuild it for us. I asked her how much we had in our savings and she answered $9,500.00 but she also said that she was happy with our house especially since the remodel and did not want to move. Not very happy, I told her even if we didn't live in it we could purchase it, I could rebuild it, sell it and make a very good profit. We continued discussing the next morning at breakfast and I proposed offering $11,500.00 cash and borrowing the $2,000.00 from her stepmother. We had borrowed from her before and paid it back within a year. I had also heard through the grapevine that he had to come up with $10,000.00 cash for a business that he had gotten into. I mulled it over at lunch and since we had an agreement that after we had both discussed a matter that I could make the final decision. I took into account her concerns about borrowing money, so I told her when I got home that I thought that we should offer him $9,500.00 cash and if he takes that we have a deal and if doesn't I would accept it end of subject. I called him and made the offer. He said Hell no. I accepted it. Then three weeks later he called and said if we were still interested to meet him at the Title Company.

Then I met with a draft person, Barbara White and made changes including a beam ceiling over the kitchen, living room and dining room. The roof was extended over the existing open deck. I got the permit and started the tearing out of the building and then rebuilding with trade labor with several contractors and hiring our carpenters to help with the roof beams and rafters. I worked on the house myself for almost a year and when I was almost finished with the house when I asked her to bring the kids out on a Sunday for lunch on the covered deck and they really enjoyed seeing the house and the view. When I got home on Monday the kids started asking if I was going let Momma have the house. I waited until we went to bed and asked her what this was all about with the house. She said that it was really nice, she loved it and that she thought we should live there. Boy, I was happy as a peacock. We moved in May 1970 with very little furniture, but everyone was very excited.

We were both working extremely hard so during the Christmas/New Year holiday I suggested that we take a week or so off since the business was now ours. She told her sister-in-law that we were planning on taking time off and she offered their place at Tahoe Keys. We had to pick up the keys in San Francisco. We drove up the coast and stopped in Pescadero to have a contract signed for a job we were going to start. While we were there Lawrence Silva called. We had built a new home for Lawrence and he wanted us to stop by on our way out. Boy did he surprise us with a steak BBQ dinner. After the great dinner we thanked them and were off to San Francisco to pick up the keys. We got there around 7:30 and they suggested we stay the night and leave in the morning. We told them no, that we would just take our time and stop for coffee a couple times and that it was really not a problem. We did just that and arrived around midnight.

The directions were very accurate we drove right to the front entrance of the condo. There was a couple of feet of snow and the parking lot and walkway had been shoveled. We opened up the condo and turned on the downstairs lights and looked around then went back to the car where she grabbed a pair of my shoes and her make up case. She said she would go upstairs and check out the bedrooms and turn on the lights and I told her I would bring everything else in and just put it all on the couch for tonight. I brought up one load and as I was going back for another l heard a thump. I didn't really think too much of it. I went in and closed the door. The lights hadn't been turned on and there wasn't a sound. I yelled Hey Babe where are you a couple of times. There was no answer. I went up the first set of stairs to a landing, I started up the second set of stairs I saw my shoes, her make up case up a few stairs and then I saw her. She had made it to the top and she was lying face down. I turned her over, found a pillow and put it under her head, found some washcloths and wet them and put them on her forehead and tried mouth to mouth resuscitation. I ran downstairs to find a phone. I've never been so scared. I was trying to tell them where we were located, but it was impossible. I didn't even know the name of the street we were on or an address to give them. I gave her the directions and she said that they knew where we were and to turn on an outside light so they could find us. I kept running up the stairs to comfort her and then back down to check for them; don't know how many times I did this. It seemed like forever, but the paramedics finally arrived. A man and a woman. The woman tried to take her pulse and I asked her if Loraine was going to be O.K. She looked up and me and turned her head and didn't say a word. I knew it was bad. They got a chair to put her in because they could not use a gurney because of the stairs. They got to the landing and stopped. My adrenaline was flowing, I picked Loraine and the chair up by myself and proceeded down to the entry. There they put her on the gurney and into the ambulance. I followed them to the hospital and waited. Finally, the doctor came out and explained that her coronary artery had plugged. That even if she had been a patient in the hospital, they would not have been able to save her life.

I didn't know what to do and was thinking about leaving when I was told to wait for the coroner. Then he came he began asking me questions I didn't understand. Why was he asking me these questions? What is this all about? Later I, of course, realized it was just part of his job. After an hour or so he told me I was free to go. In a state of shock, I went back to the condo, cleaned it up and loaded the car. All I could think about was getting home to the kids. This was the longest, saddest drive of my life. Even though you try to understand something like this happening you never really do. There is no way to explain it. I remember asking God why, why now. I had no idea how I was going to raise the kids without Loraine or how I was going to run the business without her. I was really not paying attention to my speed. I was like a zombie. I was stopped by The CHP around the Auburn foothill area and got a speeding ticket. I got home in an unbelievable 4 ½ hours. I opened the garage door and Jo Ann came running up the driveway screaming "Why are you home. Where's Mommy." I took her upstairs and explained to her what had happened. She was only 11 and it was really hard to tell her this and to calm her down. She was petrified. Then Michael, 14 years old, came home and I had to tell him. The three of us were devastated with our grief.

By the end of the week the mortuary had transferred Loraine from Tahoe and we were finally able to have the funeral. I was very touched by the number of people that attended the funeral, especially the subcontractors and their wives. They all really respected this wonderful lady.

I don't think that Jo Ann and Michael ever actually recovered from the shock and I really can't remember when they started back to school. I do remember it took me four days to get up enough courage to finally go to the office and then had to build up the courage to put the key in the door. For the next five years I worked a lot of hours and spent a lot of time raising the kids and being involved in their activities. It was so hard. It happened at a time in life when everything was getting better and getting exciting. And then the bottom fell out. I finally realized that instead of constantly weighing the bad I had to also start weighing the good things that I had for sixteen wonderful years with Loraine. It sunk in and helped me with my life and my future.

Loraine

Chapter Fifteen

I would like to talk about my years of playing softball and baseball. It started after my senior year in High School. Jess Souza, manager of the local semi pro team Swiss Dairy called me to come try out for the team. After the first practice he told me that I had made the team as the starting left fielder. I was pretty excited as it was quite an honor to be one of the first high school players to be asked to join the team. The season started with several practice games and then our regular season of ten games started. We played teams from Watsonville, Salinas, Monterey, Hollister and San Jose, San Francisco Lucky Lagger and Fallstaff Moffit Menteca. We were over 500% the first and second years. The second season I was moved to clean-up hitter (what an honor). At the end of the second season Swiss Dairy gave up their sponsorship and we became the Santa Cruz Seahawks with John Bianco as our new manager. We played the next three years and did quite well even though we had quite a hectic schedule because we were all working. We were entered into the California State Semi Pro Championship in San Louis Obispo where we came in third place with some really exceptional players, Lou Panatoni, Bobby Jackson, Bernie Bourriague and Jess Souza.

During this time the team changed playing fields moving from Santa Cruz Field to Harvey West Park where a wooden fence had to be built and Paul got the job and I got to build it.

It was at this period of time that my marriage to Charlotte came to an end and I had to give up my son Joe Jr.

After I returned from my military duty. I was asked to play softball for the Sons of Italy and did so for the next couple of years. We had a mediocre team, but it was really fun. We wore best looking uniforms of any that I ever had throughout my ball playing years. One game I really remember we were playing against Laurel Inn and I had four hits, my best ever, three home runs and a double. The following year I was asked to play for Pacific Lumber an A League top team with one of the best local softball pitchers, Jim Mills. We also had two older World War II veterans that grew up in Davenport, Mike Demos and Silvio Tambellini. This made it very exciting for me to get to play with them. The following year we won the A League Championship and again the next year. Then I was asked to play with the Santa Cruz Merchant Town Team. I really enjoyed this team. It was very competitive, but we had a good year. It was also my last year of playing softball. I decided that I had a growing construction business I had better pay attention to and devote my time to work.

I was also asked by Dr. Ambrose Cowden if I would be interested in being the new Seahawk's Baseball Teams Manager. I was really elated to be asked and told him that I would give it my best shot. We contacted the Sentinel newspaper and placed an ad for tryouts for prospective players. A few veteran players signed up along with a few seniors from local high schools and that completed our roster. My job also included soliciting funds from local merchants to help cover some of the expenses. Dr. Cowden and Mr. Johnson from County Bank covered the rest of the expenses. I also ordered all of the equipment and hired the umpires. We played ten regular games and practice two or three times a week. Probably one of the most exciting times was when Loraine and Richard's wife Ruth would come to the games with our baby sons in their baby carriages. We averaged around 100 to 150 fans and ended up with a winning percentage. I had a great time playing with Al Young, ButchWalters, Chuck Felice, Bob Destalats, Fred McPherson, Ken Doler, Bobby Vega and my idol Joe Brovia.

JOEY

Joe started his career with the San Francisco Seals in the Pacific Coast League and then had a promotion to the Cincinnati Reds in the National League where he played part of one season as a pinch hitter. He was inducted into the Pacific Coast Hall of Fame. When he was playing for the San Francisco Seals he and Elmer Morelli showed up one Saturday when we kids were playing softball at the school yard. Elmer started pitching batting practice to Joe and we kids chased the balls. Our field was so small we ended up chasing the balls in the field above the road at the end or our ball field. We were so excited, he actually hit a few balls into the church parking lot, which was really a long way out there. To end up paying with my idol was unbelievable and even more unbelievable we both hit home runs in several games. Joe made the Pacific Coast League all-stars. They were playing a team of Major League West Coast all-stars in San Francisco. Joe's parents had four tickets to the game, but they couldn't drive. They asked my brother, Tony, if he would drive them so I got to go too. Joe had a great day at bat getting three hits in his five at bats. The West Coast all-stars included the three Dimaggio brothers, Joe, Dom and Vince. Joe Dimaggio hit a home run to center field that went halfway across the parking lot and became my second idol. I became a Yankee fan and I'm still one to this day. After watching their games all these years Derek Jeter became my third idol. The Yankee shortstop is nothing but a clean cut honest and hustling individual. More young people should use him as a role model.

The fourth year of my managing the Seahawks Joe retired. The construction company was growing I decided to quit and concentrate on my family and business. I will always cherish my fond memories of playing at this level of competition. I have some good memories and some sad ones. One good one was hitting a home run in my first at bat against a form. Seal's pitcher, Tom Seals, in a practice game in Salinas. A sad one involves a very talented high school player, Bobby Vega, that I thought would have a great future playing ball. I lost track of him for a couple of years and then one day I saw him walking by the office. One morning I ran into him and he said that he did get to try out with a team, but it didn't work out and that he was now working at the Cement Plant. I kidded him and said that the Cement Plant was my alma mater. We both had a good laugh. The next year I read that he had passed away. What a loss at such a young age.

The Seahawks lasted for one more year and then disbanded.

The house I built on Plateau.

The apartment units on Blacburn.

Chapter Sixteen

When my son, Michael, turned 9 he tried out for Little League and made the National League Dodgers team. I took him to practice and ran into his manager, John Ries, who I had played softball with and he also was one of our sub-contractors, a tile setter. John came to me and that he could sure use me as a coach helping the kids. I thought because of my experience it would not only be fun, but I could also help Michael. I did this for three years and was amazed at the way these kids developed. Then it was on to Pony League for 13 and 14 years old. The team was the Butter Cup White Socks and we ended up winning the League Championship. We had good players and we did very well, but they seemed to be lacking some fundamentals and were a little bit too cocky. The following year John retired as manager and I became the new manager of the Dodgers.

I came up with the idea of playing all of the kids every game. They needed to learn good sportsmanship and how to win or lose. I taught them fundamentals that would help them at any level – throwing properly, bunting and batting. I did this for several years and it couldn't have been more gratifying.

I saw that quite a few of my kids came from homes with only one parent due to divorces. I was grateful that they could be involved with the team. Even better it kept them out of trouble and off of the streets.

One of my players, Billy Gulledge always hit well in practice but had a hard time hitting in a game. In one game we had scored quite a few runs in the first inning and we had the bases loaded in the second inning. I called Billy out and told him he was going to pinch hit, I put my hand on his shoulder and told him that I wanted him to swing at the first pitch and the same with the second and the third. I told him it was o.k. if he struck out. He nodded and went up to bat, missed the first and I motioned for him to swing again. The next pitch he swung and hit the ball over the first base man's head and ended up with a triple driving in three runs. I'll never forget the look on his face, his dark eyes looked as big as saucers.

Eric Peterson was a big strong kid. Good fielder, hitter and very coachable. We were playing against a good hard throwing left hander I told him to choke up on the bat so that he could swing faster. He told me that he thought he could hit him. I agreed to let him try with the understanding that is he strikes out he does it my way the next time. He struck out on 3 pitches and he said next time he'd choke up. He choked up on the bat and got a hit and ended up the top hitter and made it to the All-stars. I followed his high school career while he was the team's leading hitter at Harbor High. One day I was playing golf at DeLaveaga in the late afternoon. I was on the 17th tee box when I saw a tall young man on the path between holes and he yells "Hi Coach" and I realized it was Eric. He was now 6'2" and around 200 pounds and he looked at me and said that he was still choking up on the bat when they throw hard.

I continually ran into my players and it was really ratifying to see them grown up and having adult conversations with them. I also had business dealings with a couple of them. Phil Bogel had become the manager of the local Cadillac Dealership and handled the purchase of a Cadillac for us. As we sat down to sign the papers he said "Coach, I went to my boss and I got you the best price I could get". He also told me how much he admired me for taking the time to coach them when he knew I had a business to run and a family to raise. He said that he has two children and with the hours that he works he can't even find the time to play with them. Another one is Russell Gross - I was driving down Scotts Valley Drive when I saw his name on a sign. I was close to retirement and was thinking about a property manager for our rental properties. I decided to call him. To this day he is our property manager.

Chapter Seventeen

We had a lot of work and the fact that I really liked my work helped. The three of us went on with our lives. We took turns picking a daily menu, did the laundry and cleaned the house on weekends. We had family BBQ's once a month. It seemed to be working out well for everyone. My stepdaughter, Barbara, became the office manager and we hired a new secretary. It was going pretty smoothly. Not the same as with Loraine, but it was O.K. It had to be. I still missed her terribly, and in some ways probably always will.

Joe, Jr. came to work as an apprentice carpenter. He worked with the excellent carpenters that worked for us and they really helped him. He had been working a short time when I took him on a job and the lady took one look at him with his ponytail and asked me if I was planning on leaving him there. I told her yes, he's my son and that I had to leave, but should be back in a couple of hours. If she was still concerned about him at that time, I would take him off the job. When I returned, she told me what a great worker she thought he was and it was just fine with her to leave him on the job. What great news. He ended up a fine journeyman carpenter and he stayed with the company for seven years and then decided to join his cousin who was fishing in Alaska. He did that for another two years and then he acquired his own contractor's license and is still a general contractor in Petersburg and is doing a really fine job.

JOEY

Michael started working for me during the summers of his high school years. After his graduation I tried to talk him into going to college. He had very good drafting and printing skills and I wanted him to get a degree in architecture. He only wanted to work for the construction company, so I put him to work cleaning up the jobs and he became a carpenter's helper for about one year. This was very hard work and I hoped that he would realize how hard this work was and change his mind about going to college, but once again he said he wanted to work with me. I decided to test and gave him some of the hardest jobs. Digging foundation trenches, working with the framing crew, packing lumber, tearing out jobs etc. He not only did a great job I could see he was truly interested and took orders well and listened well. I gradually increased his responsibilities and continued all through his four-year apprenticeship. After another year I took a good look at the progress of the continuing growth of the company and the teamwork that Michael and I had established and decided to take him on as a partner. I gave Michael 49% interest in the company.

Barbara and her husband Don, who was one of our carpenters, decided to move to Utah. It was around this time that I also began having problems with JoAnn. She was having problems at school, smoking etc. I tried to be firm and reprimanded her, but she took off to Utah. I called Barbara and asked her to try and stay out of this and let me raise Jo Ann, but I didn't get much help. The first time she left she called after a month and wanted to come home. It lasted for a while and then she left again. I told her this could not continue so she told me she wanted to stay in Utah. Ron, my step son, graduated from college with a CPA degree and worked for us during the summers while attending school. After graduation he got a job with Arthur Andersen, a first-class CPA firm.

My workload was still growing which was a good thing because it kept me very busy. A few times I was still working at 6:00 thoughts would go through my mind. Financially I was in great shape, but I had no one to share it with. I would really get down on myself. It was a very lonely time, but then I would say to myself "What would

Loraine say?" I knew that she would have told me to complete the job that we had started and to get going. After episodes like this I would change my attitude and get back to work.

Then I met a lady who lived in Salinas and we began dating. Because I was so busy during the week with our heavy workload, I only had the weekends available. We went to dinner and dancing and really enjoyed each other. After several months I began to think that this relationship could work out. I was so lonely and wanted someone to share my life with. I asked Jean to marry me. I realized almost immediately that I had made a really big mistake. There was no compatibility and she complained constantly about the lack of a social life and about my friends. It became clear to me that her main interest was money, she shopped constantly at high end stores. She asked me to buy her daughter a car and I did so. This went on for two years then I told her that I was extremely unhappy and that I was not going to spend any more of my life this way. I left for a golfing weekend with some of my buddies and by the time I got back home she was gone. She arrived here with a suitcase and left in a full van, according to the neighbors. She was the most selfish person I have ever known. The divorce proceedings dragged on for almost 5 years and was extremely annoying and costly, but in the end well worth it to be done with her.

Swift Street Building.

Chapter Eighteen

One of our subcontractors was Hawley's Floor Covering owned by Marvin and Linda Glover. One day Linda called and asked if she could come by and talk to me. She came over to the office to explain to me she and Marvin were getting a divorce and she was taking over the business. She told me she wanted to continue doing the work for Aliberti Construction, Inc. I told her that if she maintained the quality workmanship, met our scheduling and handled any call back reasonably then I didn't have a problem with it. After a year she called and said we were her largest account and she wanted to take me to lunch. I told her that I don't go to lunch. She told me this is what she was supposed to do for good business and that I had to let her take me to lunch to thank me. She convinced me. We went to Castagnola's restaurant and at 3:00 in the afternoon we were still talking. The owner Fred came over and asked us nicely to leave because they had to start setting up for dinner. We still had more to talk about we went to Polivio's and continued talking, had dinner and finally called it a day around midnight. Mighty long lunch for someone who never went out to lunch.

We began dating and after a year we made the decision that she move into the house with me. Shortly after she sold Hawley's to her installers and we moved her into an office at the warehouse complex on Swift Street where she began her new company Contract Interiors

JOEY

and continued to handle all of our floor covering needs. We were also in need of a secretary/office manager due to the dismissal of an employee who was caught embezzling, so Linda agreed to take on this responsibility. The challenges were huge as she had never managed a construction office before, but it didn't take her long to straighten out the mess that we had and to reorganize the office. We were so busy that Linda decided to give up all of her other contracts and work only for us. Our personal relationship grew even though we went through some rocky times. Part of our problem was that we had both just gone through divorces and were more than a little gun shy. By communicating with each other and developing trust we worked through it. We lived together for six years before she asked if we were ever going to get married. I mumbled that I didn't want to go through that again because of my marriage to Jeanie and the problems that I had with the money issue. She yelled at me that she was not interested in my "frigging" money. That she loved me for me and nothing else. I called the attorney and had a prenuptial agreement drawn up and without hesitation she signed it with the understanding that if all worked out after a few years I would throw it out. We set the date for my birthday, September 2nd, because it was Labor weekend all of the kids and grandkids could attend as well as Linda's family. We were married at the house in Scotts Valley in the gazebo overlooking the pool and the valley. This day had to be the second luckiest day in my life. First Loraine and now Linda. I'm writing this book 41 years later and I can hardly believe that my life has been as wonderful as it has been. Two out of four marriages were bad judgment on my part, but the other two wonderful Jewish women that I married made my life complete. A lesson learned that I would like to pass on is that life goes on and the times when you get down on yourself just take a moment to weigh the good as well as the bad that has happened in our life. It will make you a stronger person able to handle most anything. In Linda I had found someone I could love, trust and communicate with. Not to mislead you, life is not perfect, but if you both have these qualities and communicate you can work through or handle any problems and have a wonderful life together.

Life became happy again. Something in my mind that I thought could never happen. The business grew beyond expectations. Married life got better and better. The family accepted Linda from day one and through her continued efforts she gained everyone's respect to the point that they were calling her for advice.

Chapter Nineteen

We all had very busy schedules and the business was growing so it was really exciting to see. We grew so much that there came a time when we had to turn work down because we couldn't find the type of craftsmen that we needed. Our personal lives just kept getting better and better. We began to take long weekends to a condo in Incline Village that I had purchased in the early 70's. During the summer months we tried to take off once a month leaving Wednesday afternoon and returning on Monday. This gave us a break from the daily grind so I could work on blueprints of jobs to be bid. I would get up around 6:30 in the morning, turn on the coffee and get to work. Linda would get up 8:30ish and fix us a great breakfast and I would go back to work until 4:00. Then it was cocktail time and around 6:00 we would go out to dinner. If I had to work the next day, I went to bed early. But Linda was a poker machine addict and would go across the street to the Hyatt Casino to play. She actually did quite well. On occasion she would bring her cookbooks and cook a gourmet meal all day, just for the two of us. On the days I didn't work we played golf. One afternoon while I was working Linda was at her poker machines. I heard the front door shut and she came running up the stairs throwing 2400 $100.00 bills up into the air. It was so much fun – they went everywhere.

A good part of our social life revolved around the Marconi Club, the I.C.F., the Sons of Italy and the Piemontese Nel Mondo of San Francisco. There were BBQ's, dinner dances card games, bingo, bus trips to casinos and horse races, bocci ball, etc. Now that Michael was my partner, we were able to take longer vacations.

Our first trip was to Spain, but we only went for one week and soon realized that we should've made it longer. We played golf almost every day; I saw my first bullfight; did some wonderful shopping and ate extremely well. Our second trip was to Scotland for three weeks where we actually played golf for 17 days. It was a wonderful experience to play the old course at Saint Andrews. What an overwhelming feeling to play where it all began. We went on three cruises, have been to Bermuda, The Dominican Republic twice, Boston and all of New England, Canada, back to Spain and then to Portugal and a month-long road trip to visit all of the grand kids and great grand kids. Many trips to Hawaii including the time I took Linda there, as a surprise for her 50th birthday.

One or our most memorable trips was with Bobby and Ardilla Camarlinghi to Niagara Falls and Toronto. After a few days at Niagara Falls and then Toronto we were scheduled to take the train from Toronto through upstate New York to New York City. We had our tickets, box lunches and wine ordered to leave on September 12, 2001. How lucky for us that we weren't scheduled for September 11th, but we weren't so lucky getting out of Toronto. The border was closed so we were there for four more days before we got a train to Chicago and then we were stuck in Chicago for three more days until we finally were able to rent a van. We shipped most of our luggage and took off. We took turns driving cross country, something I had always wanted to do. We saw miles and miles of cornfields and other types of farms. We were definitely not on a pleasure or sight-seeing trip. All we could think about was the awful tragedy that had befallen our country and the lives that were lost. I know Linda cried herself to sleep every night. It took several days and many miles – could be a book in itself - but we finally made it to our Condo at Incline Village where we stayed for a couple of days to rest. Then we finally got home safe and sound.

We had an exciting trip to Miami to watch the 49ers play San Diego in the Super Bowl. We stayed out on the Keys where I was fascinated by the bridge over the Gulf that is 7 miles long. We used to go to Calistoga every year with the Camarlinghi's and sometimes the Zoccoli's and Della Santinos. For over 13 years we went with our friends the Carnevale's to Las Vegas.

But the highlight of all of our trips are the ones to Italy. Our first trip was in 1996. We went with the Piemontesi Nel Mondo of San Francisco on a tour of the Piemonte. Our tour guide was a very bright and exciting lady, Lucetta Rosetto. We started the tour at Lago Maggiore and then we took a train to Cuneo where my cousin and her family lived. We had never met before and this was a real thrill for both of us. They lived at that time on five acres in a beautiful home with a fantastic wine cellar that Marcos had built. They were both retired. He grew fruits and vegetables and when harvested what they couldn't use he took to the Mercado in the Plaza which was held every Tuesday. Roberto, their son is married to Gabriella and they have two children Francesco and Martina. We were actually there for Francesco's birth. Roberto is a train conductor and Gabriella is a schoolteacher. Their daughter, Manuela, works for the hospital as the head of Radiology. It was such a thrill, meeting family members for the first time. But an even bigger thrill was when they had us over for dinner and my mother's sister, my aunt who was in her 80's, was there. I know my heart stopped. It was different than seeing my Uncle Mike and Uncle Bob because I saw them continually. Seeing my mother's sister was almost like seeing my mom. It was very fortunate that I got to see her because she died the following year. While in Cuneo Marcos took us on a tour of the region to where Giuseppe had lived and to the house where my mother had lived and then to the one-bedroom apartment where she and Tony had lived when Giuseppe came to America. We couldn't see the inside, but from the outside you could see the door and a window with wrought iron protective covers. I will always be thankful to Marcos for taking me there.

While we were there Nucci's neighbor was having their 25th

wedding anniversary party and we were also invited. The party started at a restaurant at 12:00 noon and went on for hours with many, many courses of food. At 6:00 we went to Nucci's house and we took a nice long walk and when we came back to the neighbor's three-car garage that was turned into a party room. The party started all over again. Out came more food and Marcos brought out his accordion and the neighbor brought out his guitar along with song sheets. Around midnight Marcos asked if we wanted to go back to the Hotel and I told him "No. When it's over it's over". We were there until 2:00 A.M. What a party. Fourteen hours. The next day Marcos took us to the Mercado on the Plaza. This is huge. Many refrigerated trucks with cold cuts, salamis and big rounds of all kinds of cheeses. Marcos went up to one of them and asked for a taste of one and gave it to Linda and asked if she liked it. When she said yes she really liked it, he had the guy cut a five pound piece and this went on two more times when I poked her and said we needed to stop. He was doing this to give to us and I didn't know how in the world we were going to get it all home. Linda bought a black patent leather pair of shoes that she wore and wore until they finally gave out just last year. Pietro, the butcher, who loved my Uncle Mike gave us two salamis to take back with us. I told him that I didn't think that we could get them home, but he insisted that he had had such a good time with us that we had to take them!

We continued our trip by train to Venice. We went out onto the balcony of our room which overlooked the Grand Canal. I looked over at Linda and she had tears coming down her face and she thanked me for bringing her there. She had read about Venice and dreamt about it, but she never thought she would actually be there. We hung the two salamis in the window of our room and Linda said they looked like two penises hanging there. We have been lucky enough to go back to Venice three more times.

On our second trip to Italy, to visit the family, Marcos's sister passed away just after we arrived. Attending a funeral in Italy is truly an interesting experience. One I would rather not go through again. After we left the family this time we went to Lago di Como

– Lake Como. I had always wanted to play golf in Italy. I had the opportunity to play the golf course where the Italian Open had been played several times just outside of Como. After golf, I went out to the veranda and ordered a beer. I relaxed and enjoyed the wonderful view when a little old Italian gentleman came by walking his dog, so of course we struck up a conversation. I offered to buy him a beer and he accepted. It was so exciting for me to be able to actually converse in Italian with him. I was really late getting back to the hotel. Linda was having lunch on the patio and had ordered a nice bottle of wine to share with me. I was so late that by the time I got there most of the wine was gone. While in Como we were lucky enough to witness a closing ceremony of a youth sporting event. There were fireworks from out on the lake and the sparks actually came onto our balcony while we were watching. A great experience. There is one island on the Lake and on this island is a restaurant that we have now been too a couple of times. Lunch takes the whole afternoon and the minute the wine bottle is empty it is replaced with a new one. Among the many courses is fish from the Lake and I have never tasted such fresh fish in my life. Wonderful.

Several of our trips to Italy have been with the Piemontesi Nel Mondo from the Bay Area (San Francisco) which concentrated on Northern Italy. Our tour guide was always Lucetta Rosetto. We have actually become very good friends with her and her husband, Roberto, who was a General in the Italian Army of the Alpinis. They knew that my father was also an Alpini soldier and that he had been captured by the German Army and was a prisoner for about a year and a half. This wonderful couple took the time to research my Mom and Dad. They found a copy of their marriage certificate and found out the outfit my Dad was in and got me the correct Alpini hat for his battalion. On one of their visits to the U.S. Roberto told me that he had located the place where the battle took place when my Dad was captured and that he would take us there on our next trip to Italy. Our next trip we went first to Santa Margherita Ligure with side trips to Sestri Levante and Portofino and then took the train to Cuneo to visit the family again. Marcos had passed away and Nucci and Manuela had moved into the city of Cuneo to a town house just down the street from Roberto and Gabriella. We once again had a wonderful four-day visit with our family. Roberto and Lucetta picked us up at our hotel and off we went. We saw the barracks where my father's battalion originated from and then we went to lunch in a small village with Lucetta's father. Then we proceeded on to Venice where we stayed at the military hotel. It was really fun to stay there. At meals you are seated by rank so, of course, we were always seated at the best table because of Roberto. We had dinner with some of their friends at a typical Venetian restaurant (not a tourist spot) and had one of the most interesting meals we have ever had. After dinner we went to St. Mark's Square for an aperitif when it started raining. We have a great picture of the General holding Linda's pink umbrella over his head. We went to the mountain where my Dad was captured during World War 1. He was then held captive. Roberto explained that the first battalion at the top of this mountain and were gassed and all died. Dad was in the backup battalion at about midway up when they were surrounded by the Germans and surrendered. We stopped at a little roadside chapel and I had a feeling come over me that I can't describe. We all got out and said a prayer and I just know that my Dad was there with me.

We continued on and Roberto stopped at a bridge. He told us that he was on command here during the cold war and that midway across the bridge was Slovenia. At night he could see when the soldiers on the other side lit a cigarette and they used to yell conversations across the bridge. He said there was no way that they could've shot at each other.

We continued on and were in the middle of nowhere when we ran into a small village pub and stopped for a glass of wine. It was a very, very tiny place and there were no menus. The owner behind the bar said that he would like to fix us something to eat. We ordered wine, then he came out with a large bowl of pasta and another one with salad. The food was exceptionally good, his hospitality was wonderful. The General was talking to one of the villagers who said that they were so far from civilization that they were known as the lost village and no one even knew they were there. They took us from there to Bassano del Grappa where we toured the Alpini Museum and of course sampled the Grappa and bought some to take home.

We are forever grateful for our friendship with Lucetta and Roberto. We have returned several times to visit with them. Lucetta took us places we would never have found. Little village restaurants, the Alpini band concerts, the many Alpini forts. There is no way we can thank these two wonderful people enough. We also cherish the times that they have come here to visit. The four of us have become so very close.

The last time we went over Nucci had passed away. We visited with Roberto, Gabriella and Gabriella's mother and the kids and Manuela for four or five days when we finally talked them into planning a trip to the States for a visit. Then Roberto and Lucetta picked us up again and we stayed at the hotel in their village. Lucetta fixed Linda a Rosh Hashana dinner for the Jewish New Year. She had studied up on it to surprise her. Then we went on to Torino to join the last tour with the Piemontesi that we have taken. We do look forward to more. We have made many friends with this group. We have gone to the annual BBQ at Henry Trione's polo estate in Santa Rosa, the winery in Martinez and the bayside park in San Rafael. I would like to thank all of the people involved with the Piemontesi Nel Mondo who through the years have worked hard to put these functions and trips together.

On these many trips we went to Sicily, Sorrento, Pisa, Rome, Lucca, Naples, Genoa, Cinque Terra, Asti, Alba, Milano, Torino, Florence, the Amalfi Coast, Mount Blanc, Lucerne, Munich, Vienna, Lichtenstein and many more places that I cannot even remember the names of.

A few years back we went on a road trip to visit all of our kids. It took us two days driving to see the kids in Ogden, Utah. We stayed three days visiting with Jo Ann's kids, Waylon, his wife Brandi and great grandson Gage and Brandi and great grandson, Lawson. It was so wonderful spending time with my daughter's beautiful family.

They took us all over Ogden and surrounding area. We were very sad to leave them.

    We continued on to Yellowstone National Park where we spent two amazing days sightseeing and then left to go to Montana where we planned on playing golf and seeing more of our beautiful country. Linda was doing all of the driving since I was having eye trouble at the time and I was the navigator. Ha. We took a wrong turn out of the Park and ended up in a little burg just outside. We stopped and had a bowl of soup and got directions to Billings because we didn't want to go back through the park to exit into Montana. We left and started out on the Chief Joseph Scenic Highway and went over the Chief Joseph Pass into Wyoming. Now we took another wrong turn and ended up in Thermopolis almost out of gas and 150 miles out of our way. Because we didn't have a definite schedule this really turned out to be a great adventure. We had a nice dinner at the motel and sat outside on our patio and watched the Giants baseball game on the i pad and then went to the giant spring water hot tub and met some really interesting people. Next, we found out that we were really in the middle of nowhere and had to go back the way we came to get to Montana. We finally ended up in Bozeman which is really an interesting place. We made tee times to play golf and planned on being there for three days. Never made it to golf because it really was raining hard. We took a ride to the golf course anyway just to take a look and on the way there we saw a Boys & Girls Club. We stopped there on the way back and had a great tour of the club with the Executive Director who told us that most of the money raised was by the kids. Very interesting and informative stop. Since we were not able to play golf, we decided to go ahead and go to Helena. On our way we stopped at a Jack Nicklaus course that we wanted to play. It was really snowing (in June) and that weather was supposed to continue for a couple of days, so we only stayed one night in Helena. We got to Spokane and found a really nice place to stay and were finally able to play golf at a course we had played several years before with some friends who used to live there.

    Our next stop was Ellensburg where our granddaughter Annie

lived and went to the college there. Our grandson Sean came down from Alaska to visit and we had a great time seeing the two of them. Have some wonderful memories of our visit with them. Then we went to Ashford for our great grandson's, Dalton, graduation from High School. We rented a lovely cabin on Big Creek located at the base of Mt. Ranier and stayed and visited for five days. Linda helped Sheiska, our granddaughter, cook a Bolognese dinner for the whole family one night and another night the family, Andy (Sheiska's husband), Dalton, A.J. and the twins Emily and Joseph came for a BBQ at the cabin. We went to North Trek one day and up to Paradise for Father's Day Brunch with the whole family, including Joe, Jr. We got to see Emily and Joseph in a little school play, this was really fun. We thoroughly enjoyed the whole trip. It meant a lot to me to get to see all of these kids, especially at my age.

In 2013 we took another trip up north for Annie's graduation from College. Her mother, Elaine, was there and Sean came once again. It was so exciting to see her graduate and we were so pleased to see what a lovely young woman she had become. We had a great picnic down by the river and spent many an hour just catching up. We left after three days and drove over to Ashford again to see Sheiska, Andy and the kids. We stayed at our cabin on the creek again. Dalton was returning from his eight -month stint with the Americorp Fema Division where he helped with the Hurricane Sandy clean up, so we had another Bolognese dinner for the whole family up at Andy and Sheiska's house and another BBQ at the cabin. We love these visits to see all of them and love seeing how Emily and Joseph have grown.

Chapter Twenty

Besides all of the good things there have also been many tragedies in my life. First my mother Maria dying in childbirth having me. And, of course, the early death of my wife, Loraine. I've already told you how devastating these two deaths were to me.

I lost my Dad in 1958 at the young age of 58. I was working at the new fire house in Davenport on the corner of our Pacific Elementary School lot. I was hanging doors and windows when around 9:30 my stepmom, Caroline, came to the job and said that they had just brought Dad back from the Cement Plant and that he doesn't look too well. I picked up my tools and went to the house. He was pale and did not look good at all. I told him that I thought that I had better take him to see a doctor. He said that he would get his sweater. I knew then that it must be bad for him to agree to going. When I got him to there the doctor sent him immediately by ambulance to the hospital. Loraine, my brother Tony and his wife, Lola, and I went to visit him. Even though he had many tubes connected to his arm, he was able to sit up and talk to us. They said that he had had a stroke. We stayed an hour visiting and left. I got the phone call the next morning at 5:00 a.m. that he had another severe stroke and died. It seemed that he died quickly when he was still so young. I was 28 and tried to analyze our lives together. I would never forgive him for the beatings he gave, but I give him credit for

JOEY

working hard, raising Tony and me, putting a roof over our heads, the cooking, raising all the animals and his wonderful garden. We never had much money, but we always had food and plenty of it. I think at least I made him happy with what I had accomplished and that I was actually amounting to something.

On Saint Patricks Day in 1988 I lost my brother, Tony, to cancer. He had bone cancer that was originally misdiagnosed for a three-month period. Then they found that the cancer had progressed too far for any treatment. He went home with only Lola to take care of him. Her main concern was changing the sheets daily for him for he was now bed ridden. I arrived every day at 4:30 to help her. I would then stay and talk with him about our growing up together and some of the good times we did have. I felt very blessed to have this time with him. This lasted for around six weeks and then Hospice came in to help and to console Lola. Lola called at 5:00 the morning of March 17, 1988 to tell me that he had died. We went over there immediately. Tony had requested that he go out feet first. The mortician came, I asked him to please take him out feet first and he did. I was now the only one left in our little family.

In 1992 Linda's mother, Carolyn, was diagnosed with Alzheimer's disease and she went to Texas to help her Dad put her into a home in Dallas. We visited her several times before she died in 1997. We lost her twice. Once to the awful disease and then when she died.

My grandson Nathan was adopted by Michael and his wife Kathy. He was born prematurely in Children's Hospital in Oakland. He, unfortunately, was born with Cerebral Palsy and Asbergers (a form of autism). He was confined to a wheelchair. Mike worked and Kathy was the complete care giver for Nathan. No mother could have loved a child more. She treated him as a normal child and even had him enrolled in public school. He was a beautiful child, bright, loved his Mario games. When they came to our house for BBQ's I would fix his favorite – steaks. He always would ask "what are you barbecuing Gramps". He wasn't very fond of vegetables, but he sure loved his meat and mashed potatoes. He had a special name for Grandma Linda – Princess Leia.

In 1990 Kathy was diagnosed with Leukemia. She was hospitalized immediately and was even sent to Stanford for a bone marrow transplant. She went into remission for a very short period of time and then after this two-year battle with the awful disease she died. Once again someone died at a very young age. This left Michael as the only care giver. It was a good thing we were a family business, so he was able to spend quite a bit of time first attending to Kathy and then to Nathan. I can only guess how difficult this was for him. My heart went out to him knowing I had been through the same thing when I lost Loraine.

Michael remarried a couple of years later to Candace who worked for the county, working with children with disabilities. After several years and with her expertise they were able to find The Woods School in Pennsylvania for children with similar disabilities as Nathan. Our Nathan left for this school in 1999. He was 13 and happy and enjoying the other children with similar disabilities.

Because of many years wheelchair he had developed severe scoliosis and the Doctors recommended surgery to put a rod in his spine to prevent further curvature. They said that at his age it would be the perfect time to do this. Mike and Candy went to Pennsylvania for the surgery. He was taken out of intensive care and was doing fine, so Michael came home and left Candy there with Nate. Michael called us when he returned to give us the good news. Then around 4:00 a.m. on August 2, 1999 we received the call from him that Nathan had died. During the night Nathan rang for the nurse and told her that he needed air. He meant that he couldn't breathe, she thought he wanted the air conditioning adjusted, so she gave him a Tylenol and turned downed the air and left him. When she went back to check him, he had died. It appears that during the operation the diaphragm was punctured causing congestive heart failure. We were in complete shock. I couldn't even begin to imagine what Michael was going through. He lost his wife and now his son. Our hearts were broken once again.

Just after we lost our Nathan Linda's farther, Allen, had a severe stroke. Linda left immediately for Texas and spent a week there

JOEY

settling his affairs, cleaning out his apartment and finding a home for his two dogs. She and her brother faced the terrible fact that he was in a coma and would never recover and had to make the decision to take him off of life support. He died a week later.

The next tragedy in my life is not a very easy thing for me to talk about. I told you earlier about Jo Ann and how she continually ran off to Barbara's in Utah. She continued to lead a troubled life. Not too long out of high school she married Rusty Long and had a son, Waylon. Then they had a daughter, Brandi. They struggled for several years in Utah and then decided to move to Santa Cruz to try to make a new start. They moved into the home I had built for Loraine's parents. Rusty went to work as a painter for L & M Fine Painting. The L in the name was for Linda who was a partner with the painter Mike Petty. Jo Ann started working with Linda to learn the floor covering business. The intent was for Rusty to eventually become a partner with Mike and for Jo Ann to take over the floor covering business when Linda retired. We never really understood why this all didn't happen, but Jo Ann had more problems. The most serious of which was her alcohol abuse. We had an intervention done that failed miserably and shortly thereafter they packed up and returned to Utah. All communication broke down. I finally told her that when she was ready for help to call me. After six months I received a call that she was ready for help. After Linda did some research and with her brothers help, she found one of the first alcohol abuse centers located in Fort Worth.

We flew Jo Ann and Rusty to Texas and we met them there. We stayed for one week and Jo Ann was there for a month. We were both extremely pleased with the program and with the leader Lou Bascalia. Jo Ann completed the program with wonderful results. I was extremely proud at the end of her first year when she gave me her one-year sobriety certificate for my birthday. She went to work for I.R.S. and she and Rusty were in the process of renovating a duplex to live in. We were communicating and life seemed to be improving for them. One day she called and told me that the city of Ogden had seized a property from someone who had been involved in drug trafficking. She described the property and said that it consisted of a two-story Victorian house and another three-bedroom dwelling and a bachelor suite and that the starting bid would be $88,000.00. This sounded too good to be true. We flew to Ogden to check it out. Everything looked a lot better than I expected. Since they did not qualify for a bank loan, we decided to loan them the money from my retirement fund. She only wanted to bid the $88,000. I told her that I didn't think they would get it at that price and to bid at least $95,000.00. Lo and behold they got the property and there was only one other bidder that did bid the $88,000. They moved into the three-bedroom lower floor of the Victorian and rented their duplex and then they had the three-bedroom house as additional rental income. In fact, Brandi and my great grandson Lawson now live on this property.

Her sobriety continued for approximately 10 years. In 1989 Jo Ann, Rusty and the kids and Mike, Kathy and Nathan all came to our condo in Palm Springs for Christmas. Their Christmas present was a trip to Disneyland. We spent two wonderful days with all of them at Disneyland. Brandi drove us nuts singing "It's a Small World" over and over.

Just after this trip Waylon was playing at a friend's house when they somehow found the fathers gun. While playing with it, Waylon was shot in the stomach. Yet another trying time in the Aliberti family. He recovered from this and is now a wonderful dad himself. Jo Ann seemed to handle this episode quite well.

Then there were gradual signs that things weren't right with Jo Ann. There were temperamental flare-ups and our communication had deteriorated. As a parent you can sense when something is wrong, even though she kept telling me everything was fine. She was only telling me what she thought I wanted to hear and what she wanted me to know. It went from bad to worse, she and Rusty filed for divorce and all communications stopped. After quite a while she did call to say that the divorce was final and that Rusty had bought out her share of the property and he in turn paid us what was due. She purchased a condo and a new car with her money. About a year later she called from another state and said that she was having the enamel scraped on her teeth. A couple of days later she called and needed money to leave there, so we took care of this. A week later I got a phone call telling me she had talked to Barbara and she wanted to come to California to get help, but she didn't tell me what for. I told her that I would make sure she got whatever help she needed. She told me "I love you Dad". Those were her last words to me. On October 13, 2000 she left for California with two girlfriends. They stopped over in Reno, Nevada. The two girls left the room to go down to the casino. When they returned a few hours later, they found her with a plastic bag over her head; a candle lit and a picture of Loraine on the pillow next to her. We lost our beautiful daughter at 40 years of age. We had a private ceremony for family only and per her wishes she was cremated. Her ashes were spread out to sea at Davenport. When we received the autopsy report we saw the evidence of drug abuse. All I can say is that I have learned that with the bad there is always something good. It doesn't change anything, but I honestly think it helped me get through this. That and Linda and I had each other to lean on. The one thing that I would like to pass on is that at times when I think of the hardships that have occurred in my life, I also always try to weigh the wonderful things that have happened. Nothing can be changed, but it helps me to continue on and I hope that this thought can help others as well. I also keep remembering what I felt Loraine say. "You better get with it and finish the job we both started".

Chapter Twentyone

When I was getting close to retirement, we decided that we would like to spend our winters in a warmer climate. We visited Arizona, San Diego and even spent 10 days visiting private clubs all the way down to San Diego and then up the coast. We finally ended up looking at locations in the Coachella Valley and after we spent a week in Palm Desert with friends, Maureen and Norman Benito, we bought a condo in Cathedral Canyon Country Club in Cathedral City. We spent several weeks annually there and also rented it out for several months. After a few years and closer to retirement we decided that we wanted to move further east to La Quinta and wanted a home instead of a condo. After several months looking we bought a home in 1999 on the Dunes Course and our membership in the Citrus Club at La Quinta Resort. This membership entitled us to three courses, the Dunes, the Mountain and the Citrus Course. Then in 2004 we moved to a home on the Citrus Course, which also had a two-room casita. This worked out great for visiting family and friends. We spent six months there and six months at our Scotts Valley home. We enjoyed the best of two worlds.

The Citrus Club has both a men's golf association and a women's association. We enjoyed great tournaments and wonderful camaraderie with fellow members. Most of our fiends there were retired and are enjoying a new life with new friends. The club also offered wonderful social events including the season opening and closing parties and, our favorite, Tuesday night dining which we attended with our friends, the Brehm's and others. They have had wine tasting dinners, mystery dinners and many other themed dinners that we have really enjoyed.

Our Thanksgivings became a very special time for us. My sister-in law, Lola, and her grandson Paul came down and stayed with us for the week. Our Thanksgiving dinner was called the "Orphans Dinner" because we always had our friends who did not have family in the area or family that came for the holiday. We had as few as eight and as many as twenty-six. Everyone brought a part of the dinner. The day after Paul helped Linda put up the Christmas Tree and the many decorations.

For Christmas we always had a Prime Rib dinner with Marty, Barbara and Andrew Brehm and again friends who were without family.

Linda and Alison Adcock spent two days every year preparing the food for our Passover Seder. Vince and Alison have co-hosted this with us for many years with Alison's cousins husband leading the Seder for us. Again, we have had as many as twenty attend this wonderful event.

Mike and Sandy Morrison held an annual New Year's Day party and Sandy prepared a traditional pork roast and sauerkraut. The Brehm's hosted an annual Saint Patricks' Day party. Barbara prepared all of the traditional dishes, corned beef, cabbage, potatoes, carrots and soda bread.

We hosted an annual Pizza Party that grew to over 75 people. Our friends Mark and Rhonda Carnevale catered this from their restaurant "Nicolino's" in Cathedral City. This was really a fun party and even our great grandson Dalton has attended. People called this the real "Season Ending Party". We had it towards the end of April on a Sunday afternoon. Some people came directly from golf in their golf carts. A really fun outdoor party with lots of food and, of course, booze.

There were many, many more social events. Everyone really

loved being retired. Everyone worked hard all their lives and are now enjoying their lives.

Many of our friends from the Desert have visited us at our home in Scotts Valley. This is always such a pleasure. Many came for my 75th, 80th and 85th birthday parties. We have also visited our friends at their homes. We visited Cheryl and Marty O'Brien in Kelowna B.C., Sue and Pat Williams in West Vancouver a couple of times, Barbara and Jim Drotter in Bend, Oregon several times. One exciting trip was to visit Barbara and Pete Neroni in Dayton, Ohio. Debra and Paul Bertke live across the river from Cincinnati in Fort Mitchell, Kentucky and they came over to Dayton for dinner and the next morning we all headed over to stay with the Bertke's. We all went to Lexington to Keeneland Racetrack, sat in the V.I.P. section. It was fabulous. I decided on one race to bet on a horse named "Joey" – a real long shot. When he won everyone thought that I knew what I was doing. Only bet on him because of the name, of course, but it turned out really great.

The Brehm's bought a 45 feet yacht that had been made in the Lake Como region of Italy by a company named Granche which means crab. Marty invited me to go with him to take the yacht from Fort Lauderdale to Savanah through the Intercoastal Waterway. This trip took us one week and we had such a great time, even ran it aground once. Ate well, drank well and got to see a lot of scenery. The following year Linda and I went back and spent a week with them moving the boat from Savanah to River Dunes Marina close to Oriental, North Carolina. This was such a great trip. We returned the following year and traveled up and down the Intercoastal Water way spending most of our time in Wrightsville Beach. We have very fond memories of these trips.

After over 30 years of living part time in the desert, we decided it was time to sell our home there and live in Scotts Valley full time. We had both reached an age when golf was no longer an option and the two-day trips back and forth were getting harder for us to manage.

Chapter Twentytwo

I would just like to recap my years of working. I started working at the age of twelve at the Davenport packing shed, worked summer jobs at Brussels sprout ranches and my senior year in high school at Big Creek Lumber Mill on the green chain. Then I started working as a carpenter's helper at the Santa Cruz Portland Cement Plant and this is when I decided what I wanted to do for the rest of my life. Two years in the Army back to the cement plant and then a third-year apprentice. My first union job was working on the bridge on Highway One over the San Lorenzo River for three months and then went to work for Paul. I believe that working for a small contractor enabled me to learn faster and to learn from start to finish about building custom homes. I learned to take plans home to analyze the next day's work. I learned how to cut a roof by building an L-shaped doghouse. I learned how to cut ceiling moldings and I took home scraps to practice with. I bought a $100.00 cast iron miter box and hand saw and became a top-notch finish carpenter. If and when it rained, I had plenty of work to do inside. I learned how to run the work and how to place the crews to try and make the most money. I learned how important good P.R. was in working with the customers. I learned that if you want to be successful you need to expand.

I hired the best carpenters that I had worked with along the way. I also hired young men who started working clean up and if they were good workers, I put them in the Apprenticeship Program. I built a good base of sub trade contractors. This actually amounted to two sets of subs. One to bid the smaller jobs and the second for the larger jobs. Scheduling was a top priority. The secretary called at least a week ahead to schedule a subcontractor to do their job. I did not tolerate poor excuses for not keeping to our schedule. If they could not keep the schedule, I found another sub to take their place. Our suppliers and subs got paid on or by the tenth of every month and we never missed a discount. I hardly ever missed an appointment, and I would personally make a punch list and set the time for me to meet with a sub-contractor to complete, get signed off and get final payment. This eliminated any call backs. I took great pride in bidding and treated all customers equal no matter the size of the job. I personally checked the jobs progress and maintained a great P.R. with the customers. My day started at the office at 6:45 when I put the coffee on. Read the sports page until the crew came in at 7:30. By following these work ethics my little company grew from $200,000.00 annually to $2,500,000.00 annually. We put up a 2 ½ 'x 3' bulletin board in the front office where we put all of the thank you letters and notes that we received from our customers. By the time I retired it was at least five "deep with the letters and notes.

During my 35 years in the Construction Industry my company went through three rough economies. I recommend that in order to get through these times you need to build up a reserve account when business is going well. This will help you get through. It will relieve a lot of pressure.

I had a great office staff overseen by Linda. I had a wonderful "Mister Everything", Adolf Magee who took care of picking up material, lumber, hardware etc. and would have it ready for the crews which eliminated a journeyman's running around. He took care of keeping all of the tools and equipment in order and kept the shop spic and span. He saw that all the vehicles were serviced. Two of our more outstanding sub-contractors were Dave Sanderson, electrical contractor and Mike Petti, painting contractor. Dave would call every Monday to check his schedule for the week. We helped Mike start his own business and in my opinion the painting was probably the most important of all. When the painting is done the rest of the work can be completed and then Mike would go in and follow up with any touch up work. He never missed a schedule. Another one of my important subs was Don Moore, later know as Malcolm. He was one of the most consistent bidders of all. We became partners in a couple of business ventures, and we were also golfing buddies.

You cannot expect everything to go as smoothly as you plan. There are times you'll find someone very difficult to work with. When this happens you just need to go the extreme to do a good job and get it done and move on. When asked to bid I found it helpful to ask who else was bidding the job. I also found it helpful to supply references from prior customers. A good set of plans and specifications assured that all bidders were on the same page. I mention all of this because after doing this for many years and many jobs I have heard many horror stories. I also would like to point out that it is impossible to get first class work at a cheap price.

One of the most challenging jobs I did came after I had been in business a very short time. A group of attorneys, Jerry Stanley, Ray Scott, Harry Coolidge and Tom Prosser, were looking at a two-story stucco building on Center Street. They had a preliminary skin drawing that added 2 decks on the front and right elevation and a Monterey roof over the decks and arches. No actual floor plan for the interior just discussion. They wanted to buy the property if it fell within range of what they had in mind. I explained that this would be pretty hard to do at this point, but that I would give them a number and that it would be within 15% to 20% of the actual figure and that was the best I could probably do. This was on a Friday and they wanted a figure by Monday. I spent Saturday and Sunday from 7:00 to 7:00 and I felt comfortable with the number I came up with. I reminded them about the 20% and they said that if everything checks out including the purchase price that I would have the job. In a week they called and said that they had purchased the property and were able to get the permit without a set of plans. Can you believe it? We agreed on a Time and Material contract including profit and overhead. I started with the demolition and then we laid out each office and a secretary and reception area. I cut templates for the arches for their approval and met with each one for each office for approval. I also had approval for the wrought iron and false ceiling beam. I got the job done on time with both sides happy and I was actually within a 10% margin of my estimate.

We had another challenging job with Marty and Judy Hernandez on Hollins Drive in Pasatiempo. They had a 4500 sq ft house that was destroyed by fire and had to be demolished and rebuild. We got a wonderful thank you note upon completion. They were so pleased they offered to let us bring any future customers to see the job if they wanted references.

Bob Warne, Insurance Adjuster, called us right after the 1989 earthquake and said he had an urgent problem that I needed to take care of immediately. It was the Driscoll family home on Brown Valley Road in Watsonville. The dwelling was two stories and was located on the edge of a high peak. The upper left foundation failed, and the aftershocks were causing movement and slipping downhill. Because of the steepness it was impossible to shore. I suggested that we get a house mover first thing in the morning. We shored up the upper level and moved it over to the lawn area. We replaced and rebuilt the lower level and then moved the upper floor back. The adjuster and Insurance Company were pleased as well as the owners and our happy firm. I think as you look at the picture it will point out the difficulty of this job. We did this job in 1989 and took this picture 24 years later and I must say it still looks great.

Another challenging job was a fire damage that wiped out the sacristy that was connected to the Saint Patrick's Catholic Church in Watsonville. The fire burned a couple of the fancy roof trusses and the Church committee decided that they wanted to replace the entire plaster ceiling with a sheetrock ceiling. The scaffolding alone for this job was $12,000.00. Replacing this ceiling was quite a challenge since they wanted to continue their Sunday Services. In order to make this happen we put a double layer of Visqueen on the complete scaffolding from the peak to the wall at the low end. We put a 24 ' sono tube from the bottom of the scaffold through a side entrance door to remove all plaster debris and it worked great. We could not prevent the fine dust from entering the church. We would stop work on Thursdays and the cleaning crew cleaned up on Fridays, so they were able to continue with their Sunday services. The committee directed us to a company that could replace the damaged stain glass windows and they did a wonderful job. We needed to match the scroll moldings on the arch support beans. We took off the non-damaged set of beams and put them on plywood and took them to the mill and cabinet shop who also did a wonderful job. We reinstalled them and it was a perfect match. This whole job ran around $700,000.00 and we had three meetings with the committee and with their final payment they included a wonderful thank you letter.

We repaired a couple of dwellings that were damaged by large fir trees that fell on the dwellings. One was a two -story L shaped home in Scotts Valley by the old Bethany College. The tree came down from the hill above the house and crunched the L portion through to the ground. Another was in Felton that fell through the middle of the kitchen and hit so hard that the stove and cook top were flattened and looked like a pancake.

We also rebuilt the historical recreation hall for the Calvary Church in Santa Cruz due to fire damage. The church is over 100 years old and on the Historical Society list. So, we had to replace the room completely to match the existing building. They also were very happy with the finished project and with our company. I was very happy with our crew, sub-contractors and suppliers. See picture.

All of this Insurance work helped fill the void in the winter months caused by the heavy amount of rain that we would get from November through February. We had fires from Christmas tree lights, wood stoves that did not have a properly installed flue and the fallen trees and tree limbs caused by heavy windstorms. There was a fierce windstorm one year that caused damage to many fiberglass patios and fences. We received 35 calls in two days. We had a freak snowstorm that caused many trees to snap. It took us three months to complete the many repairs. Then many years of severe winter rains and mud slides and flooding creating more calls than we could handle. And then, of course, the 1989 Loma Prieta earthquake which brought us more than a year's worth of work. We upset many people because we were too busy to take on any more work.

We built many custom homes and did many remodels throughout Santa Cruz County and even in San Mateo County along the Coast Highway above Pidgeon Point and in the town of Pescadero. I loved working in Pescadero where the people were down home country folks. There were no contracts mostly just a handshake. The first house I built there was for Lawrence and Mary Silva that included a horse barn. Then a house for Joe Muzzi and family along the coast. And then the Duarte Family. I worked with the mother Emma and her son Ron. They have a restaurant and bar with living quarters above. We added a walk-in box cooler room, then remodeled the complete living area above, then we built three duplex apartments down the street and converted a two-story Victorian dwelling into two units. The restaurant serves what I would call home style cooking. It is now being run by the third generation and I believe most of the menu is still the original menu. I still go up there for lunch whenever I can.

We did a lot of work for people that Jack Rich, who was a realtor, recommended us to. We even built a home for his daughter and son-in-law. Then the coastal commission came into being and their jurisdiction extended five miles inland and changed the permit process to many months. Because of this we were basically forced to abandon working for these wonderful people. It was taking too many trips up to Redwood City to work with the planning department to acquire a permit and decreased our volume of work.

We did several larger jobs. One was a project in Watsonville a tract of duplexes on forty-two lots called Park Marin. We completed 31 units in the first two years and the rest of the lots had to be put on hold due to the interest rates increasing to 22%. I was the general partner with six limited partners who were all C.P.A.'s. There were still six duplexes left to sell so my C.P.A. Pearl Rosenthal worked out a deal where they each would take one duplex, and since I had not been paid, I would take the eleven remaining lots valued at $25,000.00

each and the remaining debt on the lots of $150,000.00. The lots were located at the upper entrance with three in a row and two culdesac's with four lots each. I sold the three at the upper entrance and kept the others. After a few years I sold the rest of them for $65,000.00 each, so I ended up just fine.

When you enter Santa Cruz from the north on Highway One, which becomes Mission Street, you drive through what we kiddingly call "Joey's Arches". We added another warehouse on the property on Swift Street and then a strip mall for Larry Wolfsen, which included two buildings on Mission Street. Across the street we built the Mission Inn Motel, 42 units and then we added 10 more units two years later. Next to the Wolfsen strip mall we built a 16,000 sq ft strip mall which included the New Leaf Market and several other tenants. Around the corner on Fair Avenue, we built a three-story mini storage 67,000 sq ft with two elevators for Crockers Lockers (this led to building two more mini storages for them, one in Monterey which was also three floors 75,000 sq ft and one in San Jose that was seven buildings 90,000 sq ft). We built an auto repair shop for Chuck Fanucci around the corner from our building.

There were two jobs that I really wanted to do. The first one was for a professor, Dr. Curtis and his wife. They had purchased a couple of acres in Bonny Doon, and they had laid out, with rocks, a half octagon house out on a knoll. I helped them with the design for the roof and built the house – it looked like it grew right out of the knoll. The second was the DeLaveaga Golf Course driving range and cart barn – two floors. Since there was so little work available at this time there were 11 bidders for this job. I really had to alter my bidding process and we fortunately got the job.

There were also two jobs that I really wanted that we didn't get. One was a large dwelling fire in Pasatiempo. We were the low bidder, but we were not given the job. I went to Bob Warne's office since he was the adjuster handling this job and I guess I sounded off a bit because I was so disappointed since I had done quite a lot of work for him. He let me finish and told me to sit down. He said that the bids were close and even though I was the low bidder the company allowed them to make the choice of choosing the other contractor. He ended by saying that he could only recommend me and that he can't give me the job. We had a wonderful working relationship and we kept it strictly business for twenty plus years. He was strict, but he was also the most knowledgeable and fair adjuster I have ever had the pleasure to work with. When we had the 1989 earthquake two fireplace chimneys were damaged and needed replacing. I did the work for him and never sent him a bill. I saw him a couple of times in the next few months and both times he asked about a bill. I told him that now that he was retired, I was able to do this for him to thank him for all of the work he steered my way. It had helped me raise my family and I told him that he was not ever going to get a bill. I could not have been more pleased to be able to this for him. He was like a second Dad to me.

The second one was probably the most disappointing. It was for a classroom addition to my grammar school, Pacific Elementary. I was excited to bid it and I was determined to get it. There were many bidders at the bid opening. They read out all of the bids until they got down to last two. At this point I knew our bid was the lowest and I was getting really excited. What a disappointment, the lowest bid was $20,000.00 lower than ours. I knew there was no way they could produce the work at that price. I was shocked that the school board did accept it. I was terribly disappointed. It turned out I was right. The bid should not have been accepted as they ended up suing the contractor.

I am very proud of the bulletin board that was full of thank you notes from satisfied clients. I am also very proud of the recognition from the immigrant Italian community of Santa Cruz at the La Barranca Park and for naming our construction company as one of the successful businesses on their Park Memorial.

I would really like to thank all of our wonderful employees that worked for us through the years, all of the sub-contractors, my sons Michael and Joe Jr. and all of the many, many people that hired our company for their projects. All of these people helped to make Aliberti Construction so successful.

Chapter Twentythree

You know from reading so far that I worked really hard all my life starting at a very early age. I also learned how to save my money and I eventually got into investing and with Loraine learned about purchasing real estate. Because of these things I am at a point in my life where I can afford to give back to my communities. Linda and I have become very involved with the Boys & Girls Clubs. My interest began many years ago when I discovered the Boys Club of Santa Cruz which was located downtown on Soquel Avenue. This club became my haven after school, a place I could go to before having to catch the bus back to Davenport. Later when I became involved with Little League, I realized that around half of the kids I coached came to practice with one parent only. This was a real eye opener for me. It showed me how important it is to get more involved in trying to help these kids.

After many years I was asked to join the board of the Boys & Girls Club of Santa Cruz and stayed there for several years. One year I was in charge of getting sponsorships for their annual golf tournament. Since I had many contacts (sub-contractors, suppliers etc.) I was able to get the most sponsors ever for the golf tournament. After retirement when we bought the condo at Cathedral Canyon, I became involved with the Boys & Girls Club of Cathedral City. We were visiting with our neighbors Lloyd and Ginny Humphries who were on the operating board of the club and he told me that they had just completed a new Club building and were having many problems and issues with the building contractor. They would only come and do a few cosmetic repairs, but not address the real problems. Because it was a Boys & Girls Club, I agreed to take a look at the problems. There were way too many problems to list, but the worst was the exterior stucco job. There were cracks throughout the building, some of them one 1/8 of an inch wide. The roll up doors barely worked. I got on board and suggested a meeting and walk through with the Contractor. He seemed agreeable to making the necessary repairs and said that they would get right on it. He sent people and again all they did were cosmetic repairs and did not address the major issues at all. At our next Operating Board meeting I pointed out that he was not being sincere about taking care of the major problems and I laid out what should be done. I told them that we should get bids from other contractors for making the necessary repairs. I went to the Cathedral City Builders Exchange to get the names of local builders that would be qualified to do this type of work. I ended up with three names and did a walk through with each one with a list of all damages and repair specifications. The bids came in at a $300,000.00 range and I arranged yet another meeting with the original contractor. He was not agreeable to this at all. We hired an attorney, Robert Guililand, who brought in another contractor and the bid ended up in the same range as the others. We went to Los Angeles for an arbitration hearing where we were awarded $285,000.00. A very happy moment for me. I was so glad that I got involved. I stayed on the Board until we moved to La Quinta.

After we moved Linda became very involved with the Friends of the Boys & Girls Clubs of Coachella Valley. The Clubs of Indio, La Quinta, Desert Hot Springs, Coachella and Mecca are all under one umbrella serving 7,000 children. Linda served as the Luncheon Chair for two years, the Grand Auction co-chair for one year and President for two years. She has decorated a table at the annual Grand Table Decorating and Anniversary Luncheons with various themes for over ten years and has invited up to 30 women to join her at her table.

Through her involvement we really became aware of the wonderful service the Boys & Girls Clubs performs for the youth of America. The Clubs not only offer a safe haven for the kids at 3:00 when they get out of school until 6:00 or later when their parents pick them up after work, they also are offered a variety of programs. The programs include a computer center with a learning center to help with homework; cooking and healthy living center; art and music classes; a game room; outside basketball and Wiffle ball; a garden. They are taught how to be responsible, caring and giving citizens; character; living skills; winning and losing skills, etc. The Coachella Valley clubs have a record of very low truancy and zero pregnancy among the members.

Our home in La Quinta was on The Citrus Course at the fourteenth green and the fifteenth tee. One of the guys I play golf with went up to check out the new gazebo that we had built over a bar and barbeque area when he spotted the built-in refrigerator. He asked me when I was going stock it with drinks for them to get while they played. I told him that I would do that, but everyone would have to pay, by making a donation to the Boys & Girls Clubs of Coachella Valley. We took a coffee can and cut a hole in the lid. We wrapped a sign around the can stating that their donations were going to the Clubs. We did this for 15 years and all of the $27,000.00 went 100% to the Clubs. This was a fun project keeping this refrigerator stocked and more importantly collecting the donations. We thank everyone at the Citrus Club for their participation.

So, Linda and I decided that we wanted, upon our deaths, to give a portion of the estate to Scotts Valley and the San Lorenzo Valley for the opportunity of having their own Boys & Girls Club of the Valleys. We have given the Club $1,000,000.00 to purchase the land on Scotts Valley Drive. The property has an existing building that I renovated into a temporary club for the youth of the Valleys. Linda and I gave up our season in the desert one year to try to get this Club off the ground and running. This turned out to be quite a bit bigger project than we expected, but with the help of the communities and the Operating Board members and donations we opened the club in 2018.

The Clubs function primarily by donations from the communities, grants and endowments. We are presently looking forward to a major capital campaign. We are in the process of finding an architect to design the new building for the Club of the Valleys and at its completion the existing temporary Club will become a teen center. I have a wish that I will still be here to see this project completed. Then we would like to see Santa Cruz County and the other towns in the county come together and promote more clubs throughout the county, especially Watsonville and hopefully all work under the same umbrella as the Coachella Valley does. What concerns us the most is the drug movement and the gang involvement. We hope to be fortunate enough to get the whole County involved. Then we could be saving more young people and hiring less law enforcement. The Boys & Girls Club of the Valleys is a great start for "Great futures start here"

I once heard Barrack Obama say that everyone in some way has received government help. Well, I am sure that after you have read this book you will see why I really disagree with that statement. I started working at age 12 and continued through the summers until I completed high school. Then started in carpentry for the next seven years. Worked odd jobs on weekends in order to take care of my family and to save money so that I could become my own Contractor. All of this starting in the depression. The whole little community of Davenport was full of hard workers and almost all of them did quite well over the many years. This without any government help. This created a strong bond in the community that still exists today. There is a Davenport/Coast Road Reunion held every other year and many still attend coming from all over the United States to see old friends and trade stories.

I built up a reserve account which helped see us through the times when the economy was bad. It helped keep the company afloat. I actually knuckled down and worked harder than my employees in order to keep them working. They were the ones who helped in the success of the business and I didn't want to lose them. They all stayed until retirement which ranged from twenty to thirty years.

Again, without any government help or intervention. I didn't receive a government "Bailout".

This is my time to voice my opinions and complaints about our government. I have come to realize that the money that all of our politicians spend on elections and re-election is into the Billions. Do you really think that we are getting our monies worth? Maybe it's time for all of America to come together and put a stop to this wasteful spending. There are many months spent on campaigning instead of doing the job he/she was elected to do. Most of the monies are spent on T.V. ads where they only bash each other. It is about time they not only stop this senseless spending, but they should also reach across the aisle and start working together to get this country out of the mess that it's in.

I built up my small business of four employees and an annual volume of $200,000.00 to fourteen employees and an annual volume of over $3,000,000.00. If we were working on larger projects, we hired 10 to 20 additional employees and our volume increased. This was great, not only for the company, but helped the economy of the whole county. We needed more materials, supplies and sub-contractors who bought gas, groceries and their own materials and supplies. I helped a couple of small businesses get started, Dave Sanderson, Electrician and Mike Petti, Painter. The government didn't help do this.

Since retiring I have turned the construction warehouse into rental space. We did have eight tenants. Five were in the construction industry and they barely survived. The government did not help them. We now have just one tenant that has leased the whole property for their small Brewery. There are small businesses all over the west side of Santa Cruz, in fact I would like to point out that in our 200,000 plus population in Santa Cruz County almost all the businesses are small.

I would like for our President and our Congress to look back and see what got us here. Hard working people who asked for nothing from their country except for the freedom to do so. I would like for them to move forward and work together in running our country. Forget the entitlements, spending and gridlock which is driving our debt up for our future generations and is dividing our wonderful country. Remember "United we stand. Divided we fall."

In closing I would just like to say my life was never like the lives of the kids I grew up with. It was very different growing up without a Mom to go home to. The whole town thought that I was never going to amount to anything, especially Guiseppe. But the worm changed along the way. I learned wonderful working habits as a young man and was lucky enough to get the job at the cement plant, which started my love for carpentry. Being drafted into the Army also helped me lot. I really feel that more of our young men would benefit by serving their country in any of our armed forces. So many of them have no idea what their life is all about and have no inkling of where they want to go or do. The military would help them and guide them to a better life. It was a blessing for me to get away from my past and it gave me direction and time to think about my future. Working with Paul gave me tremendous knowledge. Of course, one of the luckiest days in my life was my marriage to Loraine. She was the first person that ever understood me, stood by me and really love me. At least I had 16 wonderful years with her and will always be thankful for that. Then my second luckiest day came when I met Linda and we are still together after 41 years.

I would like to thank all of the people that we worked for throughout the years for helping us to make Aliberti Construction, Inc. one of the most respected construction companies in our area.

I was doing a remodel for Charlie Bella and his wife at their retirement home in Santa Cruz and one day he said to me "From being one of the worst growing up, I think you grew up to be one of the best". This really meant a lot to me. Success never comes easy. It takes long, hard disciplined hours. I started investing and saving at an early age. I can remember hearing about good property investments but could not do anything about it because I didn't have the money. As soon as we did have some savings, we started looking at investment, but we always made sure that we had our own finances to back up our investments. We used caution because not all properties are a good investment. We considered location when purchasing. The benefits of investing in property are that over the years, land and the cost of building continues to increase making your investment grow. I don't think this would have happened had I not had some lucky breaks along the way and was fortunate enough to capitalize on them.

I think that the most special times for me are the times Linda and I spend together at either house, sitting outdoors, enjoying the great views and smoking a cigar or two with a cocktail, just talking about whatever is on our minds at the time. I have often said that these times of communication are the most important times in a marriage. We have been through so much together. Losing my brother Tony, Kathy, Nathan, her Mom and Dad and her brother and Jo Ann. Linda's Cardio Myopathy and my Hairy Cell Leukemia and then my own heart issues. At the end of the day, it is so important to just sit down and spend some quiet time together and not let yourself get down.

I am very proud of what I have been able to accomplish in my life and am so very pleased to be able to give back to my community by establishing the Boys & Girls Club of the Valleys. It is so important to me to not only to give back, but to leave a legacy that will live on for generations by helping youth find their way. Linda and I are in agreement that upon our deaths a portion of the estate goes to this cause as will any proceeds from this book.

Thank you for taking the time to read my story. I hope that you will be or are as happy in your life as I am in mine.

Linda and I on one of our trips

Linda and I with Rusty, Jo Ann, Kathy and Mike at Palm Springs Condo

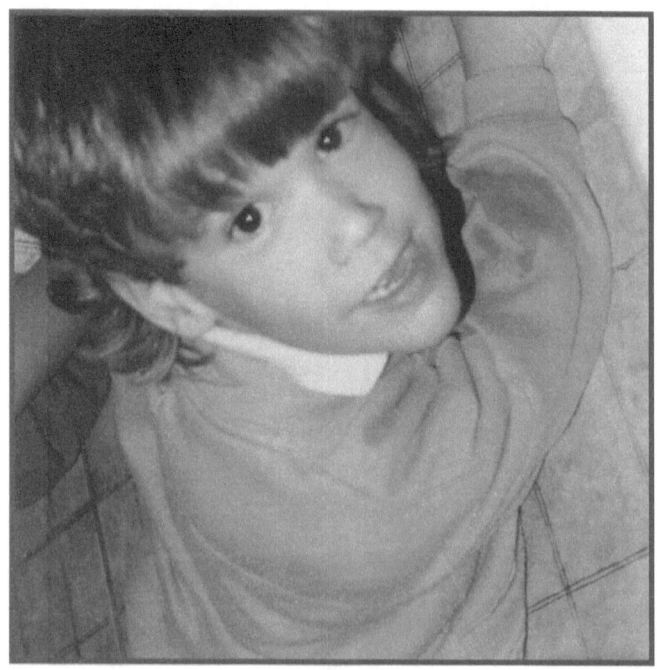

Nathan

Jo Ann, Rusty, Waylon and Brandi

La Barranca Park

Shadow Oaks Office Condo's in Scotts Valley.

The Mission Inn Motel. Part of "Joey's Arches."

The shopping center that I built for Larry Wolfsen. Part of "Joey's Arches."

The Mission Center Shopping Center on Mission Street. Part of "Joey's Arches."

My Uncle Bob, Brother Tony, Uncle Mike and Me

My cousin John, cousin Al and me

The Davenport Boys. Richard Dietz, Eddie Root, Me and Fred Moro.

Joe, Jr and Michael.

Linda and Me with Sheiska, Andy, A.J., Dalton and Colt in Seattle.

www.ingramcontent.com/pod-product-compliance
Lightning Source LLC
Chambersburg PA
CBHW021426070526
44577CB00001B/87